# IRISH HIGH CROSSES

D1113544

Bealin - East face

# Irish
# High Crosses

with the
figure sculptures explained

## Peter Harbison

✳

Illustrations by
Hilary Gilmore

PRESENTED BY
THE BOYNE VALLEY HONEY COMPANY
DROGHEDA
1994

First published in 1994 by
The Boyne Valley Honey Company

ISBN 095 1782 371

Designed: Jarlath Hayes
Typesetting: Reepro
Printed: Betaprint Ltd.

# CONTENTS

# FOREWORD
*by Lord Killanin*

Ireland can be proud of its contribution to early Christian art. From the sixth to the twelfth century, it was unique. Besides the Book of Durrow and the Book of Kells in Trinity College, and the Cathach in the Royal Irish Academy, there are many great pieces of metalwork which have been loaned to the National Museum by the Academy. Included among the artistic treasures of early Christian Ireland are the high crosses to which Peter Harbison has done full justice in this book.

I was delighted when he invited me to write the foreword to this invaluable volume, with its excellent illustrations by Hilary Gilmore of County Clare. The shafts of the high crosses were usually inscribed or carved with scenes from the Old or New Testaments or, at times, abstract designs of a Celtic nature. The high crosses are frequently known as Celtic crosses because of their circular surrounds to the top of the cross where Christ's head would normally have been, together with a halo as can be seen in the illustrations in this book.

Unfortunately, many of the crosses are made of sandstone, and I believe that they should not be left out in the open to weather in the Irish climate, as it is now possible to recreate accurate models or reproductions. I believe that one of the few really positive actions of preservation that has been taken is at Clonmacnois on the Shannon, where the crosses have been moved into the Interpretative Centre at the entrance to this most historic monument, and two of them have been replaced by accurate reproductions which now stand on the site of the originals.

Some years ago, when I was Chairman of the National Monuments Advisory Council, I learned that one of the High Crosses of Monasterboice, one of the three best examples in Ireland and located in an important area, was to be the centre-piece of the New York World Fair. The Council was totally opposed to this, and I met the then Minister of Industry and Commerce, who did not appear to realise the danger of moving the cross and the inappropriateness of putting it in a commercial context. I am glad to say that the Council had its way. The Minister was able to find a cross which had not been listed at that time as a national monument or taken into State care, and it was sent to New York where, I believe, it suffered damage. Many crosses have endured the climate for many centuries, and it is unfortunate that economics should also enter the destruction of our heritage.

It is not only the high crosses which run the risk of damage by weather. I am most anxious, for instance, about the doorway to Clonfert Cathedral, a very important Romanesque door. It needs careful protection. It is deteriorating each time I see it, and I have a series of photographs showing this. It is not practical to recreate the door of Clonfert but, certainly, every consideration should be given to its protection. This is the responsibility of the Church of Ireland, in whose hands it is. I wish I knew what the answer is to this problem.

This book is an important listing of all the Irish high crosses with figure sculpture, and is the second volume sponsored by the Boyne Valley Honey Company, who are to be congratulated on their important sponsorship of a further volume of Irish heritage. The first was 'The Treasures of the National Library', which was equally well produced. I only hope that other sponsors will be found to record our heritage. It is fortunate that the Boyne is the site of the company's products, for this area is rich in Christian remains, including Monasterboice and Mellifont, as well as those of the prehistoric era, such as Newgrange, which is as important to Ireland as Stonehenge is to Britain.

I shall certainly keep a copy of this book in my car for reference as I tour and inspect the monuments of the whole island, and I hope that many people will do likewise.

Killanin
*Chairman of The National Heritage Council*

# INTRODUCTION

The great stone High Crosses of Ireland can be mentioned in the same breath as the Book of Kells and the Ardagh Chalice as being among the greatest artistic achievements of the early Irish monastic civilisation in its broadest sense, and as one of Ireland's greatest contributions to European art of the early Middle Ages. Our respect for them can only increase when we learn to appreciate the message which they were trying to impart to those contemporaries who must have stood and knelt in wonderment before them. What distinguishes them from other crosses in these islands is the richness of their sculpture which was designed to explain the story of the Bible in picture form. The purpose of this brief guide is to elucidate as many as possible of the hundreds of biblical panels on the Irish crosses, in order to make their meaning as nearly accessible to us today as it was when they were first carved many centuries ago. Inevitably, some of the panels must remain obscure, but anyone interested in finding out more about the reasons for the identifications suggested here may delve into the author's recent book entitled *The High Crosses of Ireland* (three volumes, Bonn, 1992), of which this guide may be considered to be a much-abbreviated version. Some of its more general conclusions are summarised here on pages 11-14. The guide confines itself to those crosses which bear figure sculpture. But there are also many others which bear geometrical decoration, or none at all, and a list of these is provided in an appendix on page 109.

The main faces of the crosses normally face east or west, and are generally, though not universally, best viewed – and photographed – between noon and 2 p.m. in summer. The narrower sides are more advantageously studied in the oblique light of the early morning or evening sun. In the gazetteer, the description of the cross usually follows the sequence: east face – south side – west face – north side, and the biblical panels are normally listed from the bottom upwards. For those crosses bearing a multiplicity of biblical panels which might at first sight bewilder the onlooker, small diagrams are provided to help identify each biblical scene and its location on the cross. Where the height of a cross is given, the total measurement comprises the three main elements which go to make up the High Crosses – base, shaft and head.

9

In the gazetteer which follows, the crosses are listed in the alphabetical order of their locations. Beneath each place-name, indications are given as how to find the crosses. At first, directions are given in relation to the nearest town, if the crosses are not actually located within a town. There follows the number of the Ordnance Survey half-inch map on which the individual cross-site may be located, together with a letter identifying the appropriate square in the national grid which is indicated in diagrammatic form at the bottom of the map. Finally, there are two sets of co-ordinates to help the reader locate the cross within the appropriate square. The first set of three digits refers to the numbers (and the further one-tenth divisions of those numbers) on the left and right-hand side of the maps, while the second set of three digits refers to the divisions on the top and bottom of the maps. By these means, the visitor should be able to locate the cross to within a few hundred metres.

In addition, a map is provided on pages 110-11 showing the general location of the crosses. The appropriate square in which the cross can be found is given after the name of the place where the cross stands.

Through these indications of how to find the crosses, and the brief descriptions and discussions in the text, it is hoped that the reader will achieve a deeper appreciation of these wonderful stone monuments when he or she stands in front of them in the Irish countryside where they have stood for up to a thousand years or more.

It would not have been possible to publish this Guide without the considerable generosity and foresight of its sponsors, The Boyne Valley Honey Company of Drogheda and, in particular, its managing director, Malachy McCloskey, for whose encouragement at all stages of production the author would like to express his most heartfelt thanks. He would also like to express his deep gratitude to the Lord Killanin for having kindly agreed to write the Foreword. Furthermore, he would like to take this opportunity of expressing his appreciation to Jarlath Hayes for his inspirational book-design, to Hilary Gilmore for her beautifully executed decorational drawings, to Fergus Corcoran for his directional assistance, to Louis McConkey for his exemplary typesetting, and, finally, to Ray Lynn, Betaprint Ltd., for a fine job in printing this work – all of whom have made this book a pleasure to produce.

# HIGH CROSSES:
# HOW, WHY, WHEN AND WHERE

For a better understanding of the monuments described in this guide, some background information is necessary about how the crosses came to be, why, when, where and by whom they were erected, and what their purpose may have been.

## HOW THE CROSSES CAME TO BE

The Irish High Crosses are a product of the Irish monasteries which mushroomed all over the island during, and more particularly, after the time of St Patrick. These monasteries did not necessarily carry out the ministry practised by today's parishes, but they were great fosterers of art and architecture, encouraging the writing of manuscripts and the production of ingeniously-worked metal objects in the service of God. They were also to the forefront in studying the sacred scriptures, and the High Crosses bear eloquent testimony to the depth of the monks' studies, as they illustrate a selection of the events related in both the Old and the New Testaments, as well as in the Apocryphal Gospels. Indeed, one of the unique features of the Irish crosses is the great variety of biblical scenes which are attached to, and form an integral part of, the cross itself. The English had erected stone crosses before the Irish did, but when the Irish adopted the idea from them, they added many more biblical scenes than are to be found on English crosses.

The stone crosses we see today are unlikely to have been the earliest crosses made in Ireland. Instead, we must imagine that the stone monuments were copied from crosses, probably smaller in size, and made of other materials including wood covered with bronze, as the details of the Ahenny crosses testify. But because Celtic craftsmen had a tradition of stylising the human figure, the naturalistic figure sculpture on the Irish stone crosses must be seen as an adaptation of compositions which came from a civilisation which reproduced the human figure in the traditions of classical Greece. Rome is likely to be the ultimate source of this inspiration for the Irish crosses, but the figure sculpture may have come to our shores largely through the filter of the empire of Charlemagne and his sons in central Europe. The compositions for the biblical panels on the Irish crosses are frequently close to those found on frescoes in continental churches, and the Irish should be credited with the genius of adapting these compositions (and the tradition of classical figure carving) to the stone crosses which, almost miraculously, survive on the sites of many of the old Irish monasteries today. To heighten the effect, they may even have covered the surface of the crosses with the same kind of earth colouring used in the frescoes, though not a single trace of colouring has ever been found on the crosses.

## WHY THE CROSSES WERE ERECTED

The Irish High Crosses probably had a multiplicity of functions, including those of boundary markers, for instance, but their main purpose must have been religious. They fulfilled the same uses as the frescoes on continental churches in inducing feelings of piety in the beholder through encouraging meditation on the biblical message, concentrating on the Passion, Death and Resurrection of Christ. It is also likely that many a pilgrim knelt in front of the crosses, imbibing the message which they had to impart. Allied to this was the teaching function, educating the – probably largely illiterate – laity through a series of interlinked panels, as in a modern film strip.

The central theme of almost all the crosses bearing figure sculpture is the *Crucifixion,* which is placed at the centre of the west face of the head of the cross. Christ frequently stands at the centre of the ring – which adds that distinctive quality to the Irish crosses – and which may symbolically represent the Cosmos, the most central event in the history of which early Christians saw as being the Crucifixion. Back-to-back with this on the east face was *The Last Judgment,* which constantly reminded the beholder to lead a good Christian life if he or she were to be chosen among the elect when the final trumpet sounds.

Most of the biblical scenes on the Irish crosses can be seen as leading up to those two events and, in particular, to the *Crucifixion.* Thus, many of the Old Testament scenes, starting with *Adam and Eve,* can be understood as pre-figuring the life and death of the Saviour, including the various events of his childhood and public life and, most obviously, the Passion which led him to Calvary.

But some of the more richly sculpted crosses demonstrate that the individual scenes were also chosen to illustrate a particular aspect of church doctrine. Muiredach's Cross at Monasterboice (page 85), for instance, points to Christ as being Lord of both heaven and earth, while the Broken

Cross at Kells (page 65) brings home the message of the importance of baptism. Indeed, this sacrament is also stressed on other crosses by the unexpected introduction of scenes from the life of *St John the Baptist*. Even more unexpected are the scenes from the lives of the desert hermits *Paul and Anthony,* which were doubtless intended to impress the value of the monastic way of life. In addition, the cross at Moone (page 95) is only one of many examples where the choice of scenes was designed to show how the Lord came to the help of believers who were in peril or need, or even in danger of death.

## WHEN AND WHERE

The inscriptions present on a few crosses, some only recently deciphered, make us aware that the Irish High Crosses were erected at two different times. The majority are likely to belong to a period concentrated around the ninth century, a time when Johannes Scotus Eriugena – who graced the old Irish £5 note – showed Irish monastic learning to have been almost unparalleled anywhere in Europe. These are essentially the crosses rich in biblical themes. Those with the greatest variety of scriptural material are found in the midlands (e.g. Clonmacnois and Durrow) and in north Leinster (e.g. Kells and Monasterboice) where the series of scripture crosses is likely to have originated. But at about the same time, the North of Ireland was creating important examples at places such as Armagh and Arboe, where there tends to be a neat balance between Old and New Testament on the cross faces. Other significant local groupings include the granite crosses of the Barrow valley (e.g. Moone and Castledermot), and others in Kilkenny and Tipperary (e.g. Ahenny) which may be cognate to, but differ in style from, the midland group.

The other great period of High Cross production was the twelfth century, when the centres of creativity moved to North Munster (e.g. Cashel and Roscrea) and across the Shannon to Connacht (Tuam), though Leinster and Ulster also practised the art at places such as Glendalough and Downpatrick. The idea of starting to erect crosses again, after an interval of centuries, could even suggest an element of reviving past glories of the earlier groupings. Nevertheless, the twelfth-century crosses place less emphasis on the scriptural content, and show in high relief the figure of Christ, more often triumphant than suffering, on one face and, on the other, a bishop or abbot who probably represents the local monastic founder. The presence of the latter is likely to be a reflection of the lively pilgrimage traffic of people who came to venerate the relics of the local saint portrayed on the cross. The twelfth century, too, saw the coming of the Cistercians, but also of the Normans, and their arrival signalled the beginning of the end of the production of the crosses. However, the tradition of carving stone crosses was to continue in the form of market and wayside crosses during the later Middle Ages  commemorative crosses in the seventeenth century – and in gravestones down to our own day. Indeed, these funerary crosses of today, which reflect the rise of Irish nationalism in the mid-nineteenth century, show that the idea of the High Cross has lived on – with interruptions – since they were first mentioned in the old Irish Annals in the year 957, and first carved more than 1100 years ago.

## BY WHOM

The fact that High Crosses are found almost exclusively on the sites of early Irish monasteries is enough to show that the crosses were erected by the church authorities. But the surviving inscriptions, in as far as they are legible, show that there was also a political dimension to the erection of the crosses. Recent work by Dómhnall Ó Murchadha on the inscriptions at Kinnitty, Durrow and Clonmacnois, has brought out the names of kings who appear to have had a hand in commissioning these crosses, in particular, Maelsechnaill (846-862) and his son Flann Sinna (879-916), while the crosses at Tuam demonstrate the involvement of Turlough O Conor, king of Connacht (1119-1156). Together, they provide evidence for the co-operation of church and king in the creation of these great monuments, doubtless designed to reflect glory on the Lord Almighty, but also on the mighty earthly king as well.

One or two of the crosses may give us the name of the master-craftsman who carved the cross at the behest of the king, or abbot, or both, but the inscriptions give us no indication of his status – monk or layman. But, at least the Unfinished Cross at Kells (page 75) shows that the crosses must have been removed in large roughed-out blocks from the quarries – the locations of which remain largely unknown – and that the final carving took place only after the block was erected *in situ,* the sculptor no doubt working on scaffolding erected around the cross.

## Addergoole, Co. Galway     See map pages 110-11, square E3
6 KM WEST OF DUNMORE; O.S. ½" MAP 11.M-450.638

At present lying up against the exterior west wall of an old churchyard in the townland of Carrowntomush is the unfinished head of a twelfth-century granite High Cross, 1.40 m high, bearing the robed figure of the *crucified Christ* on one face. The other face would appear to be undecorated.

## Ahenny, Co. Tipperary     See map pages 110-11, square G5
15 KM SOUTH OF CALLAN; O.S. ½" MAP 18.S-414.290

This pair of decorative sandstone crosses, which stand in an isolated graveyard in the middle of a large field sloping down to the river which divides Munster and Leinster, have often been seen as being amongst the earliest examples in the country, datable to the eighth century. But a recent study suggested that they may be no earlier than the middle of the ninth century, which would make them roughly contemporary with some of the great scriptural crosses of North Leinster and the Irish midlands.

The crosses themselves are decorated with an intricately-carved web of geometrical and animal designs which are so similar to those on surviving bronze objects of the period that they have been interpreted as translations into stone of metalwork crosses. With the exception of one panel of human interlace on the North Cross – the one on the left as you enter the graveyard from the road – the figure sculpture on both crosses is confined to the base. The North Cross stands to a height of 3.13 m, while the South Cross is 3.90 m high.

**NORTH CROSS**
The panels on each side of the base of this cross may be thematically divided into two separate groups which are placed back to back with one another. The first panel which the visitor sees represents *Christ's Mission to the Apostles* (six of whom are shown), illustrating the words of Jesus at the end of St Matthew's Gospel: 'All power is given unto me in heaven and earth'. Back to back with it is a panel showing a man under a palm tree, accompanied by single or paired animals and birds, probably to be interpreted as *Adam being given dominion over the animals*. Taken together, the two

15

*Ahenny, North Cross - David brings decapitated Goliath to Jerusalem*

panels can thus be seen to show the hierarchy of power between God and man.

The other two panels, forming the second group, revolve around *David's battle with the giant, Goliath,* symbolising the victory of good over evil. The north face shows David riding into the fray on a chariot, while the south face illustrates his victorious return, as he bears in front of him the decapitated head of Goliath whose outsize body is ignominiously carried legs–first on a pony, with carrion-crows already gnawing at his remains.

**SOUTH CROSS**

The sculpture on the base of the nearby South Cross is in lower relief than that on the North Cross, and is correspondingly more difficult to make out, even in good oblique light. On each face, the panel is divided up into two parts by a tall ringed cross. The left-hand scene on the east side (facing towards the river) probably represents *Daniel in the Lions' Den,* while that on the right may be *The Raised Christ,* with lions above perhaps symbolising Christ as King of the Earth, as the lion was taken to be the king of animals. The other three faces show horsemen and animals, without it being possible to discern any biblical scheme.

## Arboe, Co. Tyrone     See map pages 110-11, square B6

15 KM EAST-SOUTH-EAST OF COOKSTOWN;
O.S.½" MAP 4.H.-966.756

The 'Old Cross of Ardbo', as it is locally known, stands on a gentle eminence close to the western shore of Lough Neagh, where a St Colman founded a monastery in the sixth century. Standing to a height of about 5.70 m, this sandstone cross is, after the West Cross at Monasterboice and the Moone Cross, the third tallest High Cross in Ireland. But it is also one of the few crosses in Northern Ireland which remains virtually intact, despite having been toppled apparently in a storm, after which it was re-erected in 1846.

The base has no sculpture, but the height of the cross allows for the presentation of a greater multiplicity of biblical scenes than on any other Northern Ireland cross. These are as follows:

**East face** (looking towards the Lough)

### Shaft

1. *Adam and Eve knowing their nakedness.*
2. *The Sacrifice of Isaac.*
3. *Daniel in the Lions' Den.*
4. *The Three Children in the Fiery Furnace.*

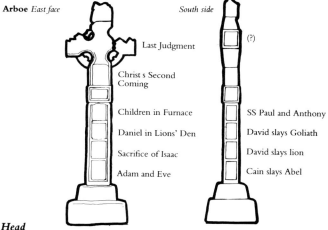

**Arboe** *East face* — **South side**

Last Judgment
Christ's Second Coming
Children in Furnace — SS Paul and Anthony
Daniel in Lions' Den — David slays Goliath
Sacrifice of Isaac — David slays lion
Adam and Eve — Cain slays Abel

(?)

### Head

**The Second Coming,** showing Christ with staff flanked by angels surmounting eleven heads. Above are the scales of Judgment licked by the flames of hell, while at the centre of the head is *Christ on the Day of Judgment,* surrounded by the good and bad souls.

## South Side

1. *Cain slays Abel.*
2. *David slays the lion.*
3. *David slays Goliath.*
4. *The raven brings bread to the desert hermits Paul and Anthony.*

The fragmentary figure at the end of the arm cannot be identified.

**West face** (the first to be seen by the approaching visitor)

*Shaft*

1. *The Adoration of the Magi.*
2. *The Marriage Feast of Cana,* with a servant pouring water into one of the six jars at the bottom of the panel.
3. *The Multiplication of the Loaves and Fishes,* with the two fish on a dish and the twelve baskets of bread beneath.
4. *Christ's Entry into Jerusalem.*

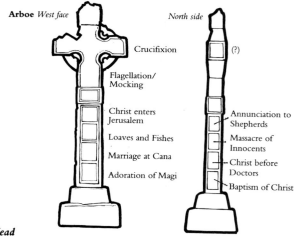

**Arboe** *West face*

Crucifixion

Flagellation/
Mocking

Christ enters
Jerusalem

Loaves and Fishes

Marriage at Cana

Adoration of Magi

*North side*

(?)

Annunciation to
Shepherds

Massacre of
Innocents

Christ before
Doctors

Baptism of Christ

*Head*

Above *The Flagellation* or *Mocking of Christ,. The Crucifixion* occupies the centre of the head, with a thief being beaten by soldiers on the end of each arm.

**North side**

1. *John the Baptist baptises Christ in the Jordan.*
2. The small figure of *the Christ child before the Doctors,* who stand beside him.
3. Two of *Herod's soldiers slaughtering a child,* which they hold upside down between them.
4. An angel with a staff announces *the birth of Christ* to the shepherds in the field.

The figure at the end of the arm cannot be identified.

★ ★ ★

The panels on the shaft of the east face give us examples of figures – Isaac, Daniel and the Three Children – saved from almost certain death through their faith in God, while other

*Arboe - Head of east face*

Old Testament figures on the south side – Abel and David – can be taken as pre-figurations of the New Testament Christ. The remainder of the cross is given over almost entirely to Christ, and provides us with a copy-book sample from the three major cycles in his life – childhood on the north side and bottom of the west face of the shaft, and then, on the remainder of that face, his public life, followed by the Passion and Death. *The Crucifixion,* an event necessitated by the *Fall of Man* on the bottom of the east face, is placed back to back with the *Second Coming* and the *Final Judgment* on the head of the east face. One unusual feature of the Arboe cross is that the scenes on the narrow north side are to be read from top to bottom. This was presumably designed to allow those who knelt in prayer in front of this side of the cross to see what must have been considered to be the most important of the scenes – *The Baptism* – straight in front of them. This emphasised the importance of the sacrament of Baptism, which is also indicated through the presence of John the Baptist scenes on one of the narrow sides of the even taller West Cross at Monasterboice, which may have acted as one of the models for the Arboe Cross, along with the Market Cross in Armagh (see below).

## Ardane, Co. Tipperary    See map pages 110–11, square G4

8.5 KM SOUTH-EAST OF TIPPERARY TOWN;
O.S. ½" MAP 18.R-946.287

In a small enclosure, off the beaten track in the Glen of Aherlow, is the head of a sandstone cross, 85 cm high, showing three scenes on one face which may be tentatively identified as follows:

North arm. *The Kiss of Judas*.

South arm. *The Flagellation* or *First Mocking of Christ*.

Top. Possibly *The Second Mocking of Christ* (or *The Ascension?*). Nearby, is the head of another cross with no figure sculpture.

## Armagh, Co. Armagh    See map pages 110–11, square C6

IN THE CENTRE OF THE CITY OF ARMAGH;
O.S. ½" MAP 8.H-874.453

St Patrick is traditionally recognised as the founder of the first church in Armagh, situated on one of the city's seven hills. At first episcopal, Armagh soon became a monastic centre which, from the eighth century onwards, claimed supremacy over all other churches in Ireland, and was the prime mover in the church reform movement of the twelfth century. St Patrick's original church was probably on the site of the present Church of Ireland Cathedral, which owes much to a nineteenth-century rebuilding. In the north-eastern corner of the Cathedral are three High Cross fragments of sandstone, known collectively as The Market Cross because they stood in the city's Market Place until they were brought inside and re-erected in their present location in 1916. The three fragments consist of the head of a cross as well as two shafts mounted one on top of the other which, however, stem from two different crosses. This can be deduced by comparing their differing thicknesses, mouldings, height of relief sculpture – and from their duplication of *The Baptism* scene. Totalling 2.34 m in height, both are treated as a single unit below.

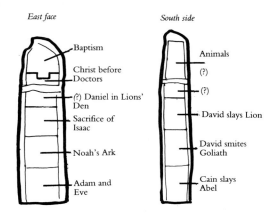

East face

Baptism

Christ before Doctors

(?) Daniel in Lions' Den

Sacrifice of Isaac

Noah's Ark

Adam and Eve

South side

Animals

(?)

(?)

David slays Lion

David smites Goliath

Cain slays Abel

**East face** (looking towards the altar)

*Lower shaft fragment*
1. *Adam and Eve.*
2. *Noah's Ark* (a Baptism symbol).
3. *The Sacrifice of Isaac.*
4. Fragmentary panel possibly representing *Daniel in the Lions' Den.*

*Upper Shaft fragment*
A damaged panel perhaps representing *Christ before the Doctors* and, above it, *The Baptism of Christ* in a composition not encountered elsewhere on the Irish crosses, whereby Christ stands in a specially lowered central part of the panel, flanked by an angel and St John the Baptist (almost obliterated).

**South side**

*Lower shaft fragment*
1. *Cain slays Abel.*
2. *David smites Goliath.*
3. *David slays the lion.*

*Upper shaft fragment*
The sculpture is not identifiable, though the animals in the upper part resemble those on the south face of the Cross of Saints Patrick and Columba at Kells (page 75).

**West face** (looking towards the back wall of the Cathedral)

*Lower shaft fragment*
1. *The angel announces the Nativity to the Shepherds.*
2. *The Adoration of the Magi,* with the Christ child sitting on the Virgin's lap, and the two bosses above representing stars.

21

Armagh Cathedral, Market Cross - East face

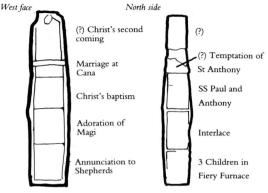

**Armagh**

*West face*

(?) Christ's second coming

Marriage at Cana

Christ's baptism

Adoration of Magi

Annunciation to Shepherds

*North side*

(?)

(?) Temptation of St Anthony

SS Paul and Anthony

Interlace

3 Children in Fiery Furnace

3. *The Baptism of Christ,* with the water lapping up to the knees of Christ and John the Baptist.
4. Six water jars at the bottom of this fragmentary panel allow an identification as *The Marriage Feast of Cana.*

### Upper shaft fragment

The carving is much worn, but the scene probably represents *The Second Coming of Christ,* as at Arboe. The large hole above is almost certainly secondary.

## North side

### Lower shaft fragment

1. *The Three Children in the Fiery Furnace.* Then, above an interlace,
2. *The raven bringing bread to Saints Paul and Anthony in the desert.*
3. A damaged panel, possibly *The Temptation of St Anthony the hermit.*

The sculpture of the upper shaft fragment is not identifiable.

### Cross-head

Adjoining these two shaft fragments is a much-worn and damaged cross-head, which may possibly have belonged to the upper of the two shaft fragments. On one face is *The Crucifixion,* with a thief on the surviving arm, while on the other face is a probable *Last Judgment,* with perhaps an angel on the surviving arm, and souls in between.

There is a further cross-fragment with no figure sculpture just inside the western gate of the Cathedral grounds.

# Banagher, Co. Offaly

SEE UNDER DUBLIN – NATIONAL MUSEUM (PAGE 52)

## Bealin, Co. Westmeath

See map pages 110-11, square E4

5.5 KM EAST-NORTH-EAST OF ATHLONE;
O.S. ½" MAP 12.N-103.429

The sandstone cross now on top of a mound not far from Bealin Post Office is probably not in its original position. 2.10 m high, it is decorated with lions, long-necked birds interlacing with one another, geometrical decoration, a horseman, dog and stag, as well as an inscription in high relief, stating that Tuathgall had the cross erected. He has been tentatively identified with a man named Tuathgall who was abbot of Clonmacnois around 800, suggesting that the cross may have been brought from there, probably around two hundred years ago.

## Boho, Co. Fermanagh

See map pages 110-11, square C4

11.5 KM WEST OF ENNISKILLEN; O.S. ½" MAP 7.H-112.462

The 2.50 m high, sandstone cross-shaft in Toneel church-yard is decorated on both faces with figure sculpture. On the east face is *Eve stretching forth her right hand to the bearded Adam*. The west face shows *The Baptism of Christ,* on top, beneath which may be *Zacharias,* with *Elizabeth holding the infant John the Baptist*. Secondary holes in the narrow sides of the cross may have held bars tied to uprights supporting a cross-head (as on St Patrick's Cross at Cashel), which was not necessarily identical with that preserved in the neighbouring Catholic church.

## Camus, Co. Derry

See map pages 110-11, square A6

4.5 KM SOUTH-EAST OF COLERAINE; O.S. ½" MAP 2.C-871.289

Standing in an old graveyard close to the river Bann, where St Comgal founded a monastery in the sixth century, is a sandstone cross-shaft, 2.60 m high which, having been knocked down in the eighteenth century, acted as a gatepost before being erected in its present position. The narrow sides are decorated with animal and geometrical ornamentation, but the two faces bear high relief figure sculpture.

### East face
1. *The Adoration of the Magi,* with the Virgin holding the Christ child on her lap flanked by two Magi on one side, and by a third Magus on the other side.
2. *The Baptism of Christ* in the waters of the Jordan.
3. *The Marriage Feast of Cana,* with six water jars at the feet of the three standing figures.
4. Probably *The Multiplication of the Loaves and Fishes*.

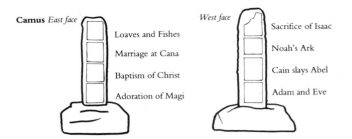

**Camus** *East face*

Loaves and Fishes

Marriage at Cana

Baptism of Christ

Adoration of Magi

*West face*

Sacrifice of Isaac

Noah's Ark

Cain slays Abel

Adam and Eve

## West face

1. *Adam and Eve.*
2. *Cain slays Abel,* with a third figure probably representing *The Lord.*
3. *Noah's Ark.*
4. *The Sacrifice of Isaac.*

The iconography of this fragment adheres closely to that of the lower shaft-fragment in Armagh (page 21) and the cross at Arboe (pages 17–18).

## Carndonagh, Co. Donegal    See map pages 110–11, square A5

1 KM SOUTH OF CARNDONAGH TOWN;
O.S. ½" MAP 1.C-463.450

Set on a plinth outside the graveyard of the town's Church of Ireland church is a cross 2.53 m high, with thick bands of interlace on the west face.

The east face (page 26) has two figured scenes on the shaft. The larger of these is *The Crucifixion,* with angels above Christ's outstretched arms. The figures beneath his arms may be the thieves, the bad thief having a bird perched on his head, while the other may have an angel in the same position. The most likely interpretation of three figures beneath the Crucifixion is *The Three Holy Women walking towards the Tomb,* a scene frequently substituted for, but indicating, *The Resurrection.* The identity of the figures on the narrow south side of the cross cannot be ascertained satisfactorily.

Beside the cross are two pillars bearing figure sculpture, and there is also a pillar in the graveyard nearby which bears a representation of the *crucified Christ.*

## Carrowmore, Co. Donegal    See map pages 110–11, square A5

12 KM NORTH-WEST OF MOVILLE; O.S. ½" MAP 2.C-516.457

Standing in a field next to the National School is a cross, 2.85 m high, which bears on the west face a *Majestas Domini (Christ in Glory),* accompanied on each side by an angel. There is what appears to be a human face on the right breast of Christ's cloak.

*Carndonagh - East face*

On the opposite side of a small roadway there is another, undecorated cross.

## Cashel, Co. Tipperary

See map pages 110-11, square G4

IN THE TOWN OF CASHEL; O.S. ½" MAP 18.S-074.408

St. Patrick's Rock in the town of Cashel is one of Ireland's most dramatic ecclesiastical sites, handed over to the Church in 1101 having served for centuries as the seat of the kings of Munster. Placed at an angle to one another on the summit of the Rock are Cormac's Chapel (1127-1134) and the larger thirteenth-century Cathedral, close to which stands an eleventh/twelfth-century Round Tower. Entrance to the Rock is through the late medieval Hall of the Vicars' Choral, now containing the twelfth-century sandstone Cross of St Patrick, which measures 4.65 m in height. It was moved inside some years ago from a position close to the north door of the Cathedral where a modern cement copy now stands, though this was not necessarily its original location. The cross is unusual in having side-supports for the arms. Each face of the cross bears one large figure in high relief. That on what was the west face is the *crucified Christ* wearing a long robe, while that on the other face is a bishop or abbot carrying a staff or crozier. This latter figure is usually identified as *St Patrick,* who is traditionally said to have baptised the local king, Oengus, on a throne which is claimed (doubtless erroneously) to have been used later as the base of the cross. This base is decorated with crosses, an 'inhabited vine-scroll' and an animal enclosed in multiple penannular rings.

*Cashel, St. Patrick's Cross - East face*

27

# Castledermot, Co. Kildare

See map pages 110-11, square F6

IN THE TOWN OF CASTLEDERMOT; O.S. ½" MAP 16.S-783.851

For a town of its size, Castledermot has a remarkable collection of ancient ecclesiastical remains. In addition to the ruins of two medieval friaries, it has a parish church (Protestant) going back to the twelfth and thirteenth centuries and, beside it, a Round Tower. But amongst the oldest of its antiquities are two granite crosses erected some time after 812, when a monastery was founded there in association with the ascetic Céle Dé reform movement. They are 3.13 m and 3.34 m in height respectively. There is also the plain base of a third cross.

## CROSS NORTH OF THE CHURCH

### East face

The base has spiral decoration interspersed with imitation nail heads.

#### Shaft and Head

1. Two unidentified figures.
2. *The raven brings bread to the desert hermits Paul and Anthony.*

At the centre of the head is *The Crucifixion* and above, below, and on each side, panels each contain three figures, who almost certainly represent *Apostles*.

### South side (facing the church)

*Christ multiplying the Loaves and Fishes* is represented on the base. The shaft bears interlaced decoration.

**Castledermot – North Cross**

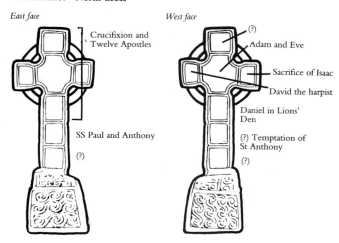

East face — Crucifixion and Twelve Apostles; SS Paul and Anthony; (?)

West face — (?); Adam and Eve; Sacrifice of Isaac; David the harpist; Daniel in Lions' Den; (?) Temptation of St Anthony; (?)

*Castledermot, North ∫ Cross – West face*

29

**West face** (looking towards the entrance to the churchyard)
The base bears spiral ornament.

### Shaft
1. Three unidentified figures.
2. (?) *The Temptation of St Anthony*.
3. *Daniel in the Lions' Den*.

### Head
At the centre is *Eve handing the apple to Adam*. On the south arm is *The Sacrifice of Isaac* and, on the other, *David playing his harp*. The scene on the uppermost limb is difficult to interpret, having one figure upside down in the middle being held by two flanking figures, of whom that on the left would appear to hold a club or a sword.

### North side
The base bears a curious crouched figure with wings, suggesting an angel. The shaft bears a spiral coil, but the figure at the end of the arm cannot be identified.

\* \* \*

Probably the most unexpected feature of this cross is the placing of *Adam and Eve* at the centre of the head on the west face. But their position back-to-back with the *crucified Christ* on the east face makes it clear that the intention was to show that it was the Original Sin of our First Parents which necessitated Christ giving his life for the human race upon the cross. *Daniel in the Lions' Den* and *The Sacrifice of Isaac* could both be interpreted as pre-figuring the Death and Resurrection of Christ. The *Apostle* figures and *The Miracle of the Loaves and Fishes* are frequently found on the crosses in the valley of the river Barrow. The *Paul and Anthony* cycle (to which the scene on the top of the west face could also have conceivably belonged) can best be explained by the fact that, in a sense, Paul and Anthony were the founders of ascetic monasticism – the kind of life to which the monks of the Céle Dé movement (to which Castledermot belonged) aspired, but also as the ideal in following the precepts of Christ as adumbrated in the New Testament.

### CROSS SOUTH OF THE CHURCH
This cross was re-erected in its present position at the end of the last century.

The east face is entirely occupied by geometrical and spiral ornament.

## South side

The base has *Christ multiplying the Loaves and Fishes*, occupying a similar position to the representation of the same scene on the North Cross. The shaft bears six panels, each with two figures who may, therefore, be interpreted as *Apostles*. The figure on the end of the arm is unidentified.

*Castledermot, South Cross – Hunting scene on base*

## West face

The base bears an attractive scene of two men hunting a variety of animals, the symbolic significance of which is unknown.

**Castledermot – South Cross**

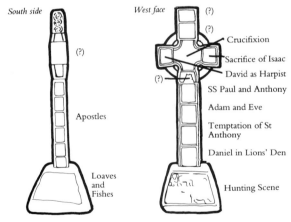

South side

(?)

Apostles

Loaves and Fishes

West face

(?)

(?)

Crucifixion

Sacrifice of Isaac

David as Harpist

SS Paul and Anthony

Adam and Eve

Temptation of St Anthony

Daniel in Lions' Den

(?)

Hunting Scene

### Shaft

1. *Daniel in the Lions' Den.*
2. *The Temptation of St Anthony.*
3. *Eve gives the apple to Adam.*
4. *The raven brings bread to Saints Paul and Anthony in the desert.*

### Head

At the centre is *The Crucifixion*. Beneath it is a damaged panel with three figures difficult to identify. The arms – like those

31

of the North Cross – bear *David with his harp* and *The Sacrifice of Isaac*. The two scenes above *The Crucifixion* are difficult to interpret. While the lower panel could conceivably represent *The Holy Women coming to the Tomb,* and the upper one *The Flagellation of Christ,* it is preferable to leave the identifications an open question.

### North side

The base has been left uncarved except for the top right-hand corner which shows two figures approaching or embracing one another – perhaps *The Kiss of Judas,* as on a scene in a similar position on the south side of the base of the Cross of the Scriptures at Clonmacnois (page 39).

### Shaft

The shaft bears five panels. The central one is taller than the rest, and shows one tall figure with sword and shield, presumably *Goliath,* with the diminutive figure of *David* beneath the sword-bearing arm. The panel beneath shows a much smaller figure astride a much larger figure seated upright on the ground, presumably representing *David's victory over Goliath.* The remainder of the panels may be taken as belonging to a David cycle, without it being possible to identify all of them satisfactorily. The figure on the end of the north arm cannot be identified.

★ ★ ★

It is the presumed David cycle on the north side which is the unusual feature of this cross. *David smiting Goliath,* the triumph of good over evil, was often taken to pre-figure Christ's victory over the devil on the cross, and *The Sacrifice of Isaac* and *Daniel in the Lions' Den* are also taken as Old Testament pre-figurations of the Death and Resurrection of Christ. If the scene above *The Crucifixion* were to represent *The Holy Women coming to the Tomb,* it would fit into the same sequence, as it was a scene used frequently in Early Christian art to represent *The Resurrection.* The *Paul and Anthony* scenes may have been particularly attractive to the monks of the ascetic Céle Dé movement and – as also on the North Cross – *The raven bringing bread to the desert*

*Castledermot, South Cross-North side*

*hermits* may have been associated with *Christ's Miracle of the Multiplication of the Loaves and Fishes.*

## Clonca, Co. Donegal

12.5 KM NORTH-WEST OF MOVILLE; O.S. ½" MAP 2.C-525.470

The cross standing 3 m high in a field to the west of the church at Clonca bears some figure sculpture on both faces, which are otherwise decorated with interlace, animal ornament and geometrical designs. The arm of the cross (with an unidentified figure on the east face) was re-attached around 1980. Beneath the head on the east face is a probable representation of *Christ performing the Miracle of the Loaves and Fishes*. The possible connection between this scene and *The raven bringing the bread to the desert hermits Paul and Anthony* was pointed out in the previous entry in a discussion of the two crosses at Castledermot, Co. Kildare. The same connection may have been intended here if the two figures shown seated on the west face were to be identified as the desert hermits *Paul and Anthony*. This is made quite likely by the presence of the two lions above them, who may be the same as those who came to assist St Anthony in digging a grave for his hermit friend St Paul, and secondly by the croziers above the lions, which are also present above the heads of the same two figures on the top of the south side of the shaft of the cross at Arboe, Co. Tyrone (page 17). The head of another cross lies in the next field further west, but it bears no figure sculpture on the visible face.

*Miracle of the Loaves and fishes on the East face at Clonca*

33

## Clones, Co. Monaghan

See map pages 110-11, square C5

IN THE CENTRE OF CLONES TOWN; O.S. ½" MAP 8.H-503.259

The foundation of the monastery at Clones goes back to the time of St Tighernach in the sixth century. His remains may lie beneath the remarkable twelfth-century stone sarcophagus situated in the shadow of the Round Tower attached to the monastery. It was presumably from their vicinity that the sandstone shaft and head of two separate High Crosses came, before they were erected one on top of the other in the Diamond, at the centre of the town. The shaft has beaded decoration and a selection of scenes which link it with the cross at Donaghmore in the neighbouring county of Tyrone (page 45). Shaft and head are treated separately below.

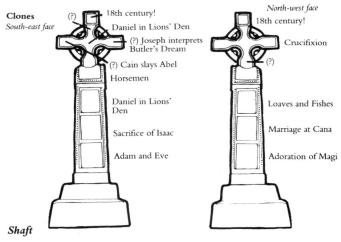

Clones
South-east face

- 18th century!
- (?) Daniel in Lions' Den
- (?) Joseph interprets Butler's Dream
- (?) Cain slays Abel
- Horsemen
- Daniel in Lions' Den
- Sacrifice of Isaac
- Adam and Eve

North-west face

- 18th century!
- Crucifixion
- (?)
- Loaves and Fishes
- Marriage at Cana
- Adoration of Magi

### Shaft

### South-east face

1. *Adam and Eve.*
2. *The Sacrifice of Isaac.*
3. *Daniel in the Lions' Den.*

The south-west side has bossed and interlaced decoration.

### North-west face

1. *The Adoration of the Magi.*
2. *The Marriage Feast of Cana.*
3. *The Multiplication of the Loaves and Fishes.*

The north-east side bears interlace.

★ ★ ★

The selection of scenes is of a kind found on a number of Ulster crosses, of which that at Armagh was probably the prime one, but the only complete example – at Arboe,

34

Co. Tyrone (page 16) – gives an indication of the scenes which were probably represented on the original head, which is missing.

### Head

The head did not belong originally to the shaft which now supports it, and the stone on the top is no earlier than the eighteenth century.

The south-east face shows *Daniel in the Lions' Den* unusually at the centre of the head, though it also occurs in the same position on the south face of the Market Cross at Kells (page 69). On the south-western arm is perhaps *Cain slaying Abel,* while the scene on the other arm resembles that of *Joseph interpreting the Butler's Dream* on the Cross of the Scriptures at Clonmacnois (page 38). The meaning of the scenes above and below Daniel is uncertain.

At the centre of the north-west face is *The Crucifixion,* with a thief occupying each arm.

★ ★ ★

The positioning of *Daniel in the Lions' Den* back-to-back with *The crucified Christ* on the cross suggests that the Daniel scene was to be seen as pre-figuring the Death and Resurrection of Christ, as would also appear to have been the case on other northern crosses, such as Arboe and Armagh. If the scene on the north-east arm is *Joseph interpreting the dream of Pharaoh's Butler,* it could also be seen in the same sense, because it prophesied the re-instatement of the Butler after three days, as Christ himself prophesied that he would rise again on the third day. *The Slaying of Abel,* as the first innocent victim of the Old Testament, looks ahead to the sacrifice of Christ, as the New Testament's innocent victim.

## Clonlea, Co. Down

See map pages 110-11, square C6

5 KM SOUTH-EAST OF NEWRY; O.S. ½" MAP 9.J-118.222

A rather isolated and not easy to find graveyard, about whose early history nothing is known, is the location of a granite cross 2.30 m high, which might possibly bear *Noah's Ark* and other Old Testament scenes on its east face, but weathering makes this uncertain. There is also a decorated base supporting a somewhat similar cross nearby.

## Clonmacnois, Co. Offaly

See map pages 110-11, square E4

11.5 KM SOUTH-SOUTH-WEST OF ATHLONE;
O.S. ½" MAP 15.N-009.307

Clonmacnois must be counted among the most important cultural centres and schools of early medieval Ireland. It was

*Clonmacnois, Cross of the Scriptures – East face*

certainly in an ideal position to receive and distribute artistic stimulus because of its cross-roads position at the very centre of Ireland where the north-south flowing Shannon river was crossed by the main east-west traffic artery, the Eiscir Riada. Founded around 545 by St Ciaran, the monastery chose its abbots for their qualities rather than for their family connections, and was thus able to keep up high standards during the almost thousand years of its active life as a monastery. From the seventh century down to our own day, it has also had a long tradition as a place where pilgrims came to venerate the relics of the founder, which were preserved in a small oratory-shrine known as Teampull Chiaráin. It lies close to the largest church on the site, the Cathedral, indicating that Clonmacnois was the centre of a diocese from the twelfth century. But Clonmacnois also has five other churches, including two in the Romanesque style (the Nuns' Church to the east of the monastic enclosure, and St Finian's with an in-built Round Tower), as well as an independent Round Tower of the eleventh/twelfth centuries. However, probably the greatest jewels of this magnetic monastery are the sandstone High Crosses which have been brought indoors to save them from the elements and which were placed on display in the new Interpretative Centre in 1993. Copies have replaced them on the sites where they stood, and their original orientation has been preserved in their new location, as can be seen by the points of the compass marked in the floor around them.

## CROSS OF THE SCRIPTURES

The first of the three crosses which the visitor to the Interpretative Centre encounters is the Cross of the Scriptures, which originally stood before the west door of the Cathedral, where a fine modern copy now stands. It is perhaps the most gracefully proportioned of all the Irish High Crosses. It gets its title because it has been identified – probably correctly – as *Cros na Screaptra,* the Cross of the Scriptures, mentioned by the Annals of the Four Masters under the year 957, and again under 1060, when people who had taken refuge around the cross were taken captive. Of the crosses surviving at Clonmacnois, it is the obvious one to lay claim to the title. It is unusual, not only for its slender proportions, but also because its arms tilt upwards, giving it a light and lofty appearance looking heavenwards to a height of 3.90 m, and because it is the only Irish High Cross where the ring predominates over the cross-shape.

Much of the discussion about this cross in recent years has

centred around the identities of persons mentioned in the very fragmentary inscriptions on the bottom of both faces of the shaft, to the detriment of discussion about the interpretation of many of the figured panels, which many scholars have been reluctant to undertake. Yet, when the cross yields up its secrets (and it has not yielded up all of them yet), it can be seen to have a rich biblical programme focussed on the Passion and post-Passion events.

### East face
This is the face which has its back to the bottom of the semi-circular ramp leading down to the cross in its new location.

#### Base
Two chariots proceed towards the right on the lower register, while three horsemen ride in the opposite direction on the upper register.

#### Shaft
On the plinth at the bottom of the shaft there is an incomplete inscription which once gave the name of the person who had the cross erected. While that person's name is incomplete to the naked eye, Dómhnall Ó Murchadha has, by means of a sponge technique, made a rubbing of the inscription which gives the text as follows:

OR DO COLMAN DORRO
. . . CROSSA AR
RIG FL.ND

which may be tentatively translated as

A prayer for Colman who
(?erected) the cross on
king Fl.nd,

probably referring to the king Flann (or Fland) Sinna, who reigned from 879 until 916. The scenes above the inscription may be tentatively identified as follows:
1. *Joseph* (left) *interprets the dream of Pharaoh's Butler,* as the two figures hold between them the budding vine which the Butler had seen in his dream.
2. *The Chief Butler* (left) *hands the drinking horn to Pharaoh.*
3. *Traditio Clavium,* Christ handing the key to Peter on the left and the Book of the New Testament to Paul on the right.

#### Head
*The Last Judgment* with Christ, carrying cross-staff and

38

**Clonmacnois – Cross of the Scriptures**

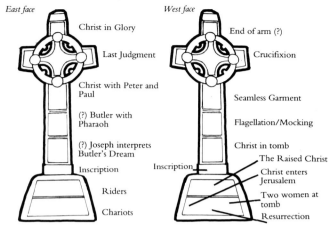

*East face*
- Christ in Glory
- Last Judgment
- Christ with Peter and Paul
- (?) Butler with Pharaoh
- (?) Joseph interprets Butler's Dream
- Inscription
- Riders
- Chariots

*West face*
- End of arm (?)
- Crucifixion
- Seamless Garment
- Flagellation/Mocking
- Christ in tomb
- The Raised Christ
- Inscription
- Christ enters Jerusalem
- Two women at tomb
- Resurrection

sceptre, flanked on the one side by a piper and the good souls turned towards him, and on the other side by a devil driving the bad souls to their eternal damnation, as they turn their backs on Christ. At the top of the cross is a panel showing *Christ in Glory,* accompanied by two angels.

## South side

The lower register of the base shows two men chasing animals to the left, while the upper register illustrates *The Kiss of Judas,* with the people bearing staffs coming from the left.

### Shaft

Above an 'inhabited vinescroll' and a human interlace, there are two panels with figure sculpture: *David* sitting on (a chair in the shape of?) an animal (lion?), *playing his lyre,* and perhaps *David as shepherd.* Under the ring two snakes enmesh two human heads, while under the arm *The Hand of God* emerges (see illustration page 40).

## West face

### Base

The lower register has much-worn figure sculpture which may be interpreted as three scenes which encapsulate the happenings of Easter Week. Reading from left to right, these may be interpreted as:

1. *Christ enters Jerusalem* on the ass, perhaps with Zacchaeus in the tree behind him.
2. *Christ rises from the tomb* over the sleeping soldiers and
3. *The angel,* with diagonal staff, sits on the horizontal tomb-slab and *greets two of the Holy Women coming to the Tomb.*

39

*Clonmacnois, Cross of the Scriptures - underside of ring and south arm*

The upper register shows *The Raised Christ* – Christ seated in the presence of three apostles on either side of him, of whom that closest to his right is probably *Peter,* though not distinguishable from the others.

### Shaft

On the plinth, the letters NDM survive from an otherwise largely obliterated inscription which Dómhnall Ó Murchadha, using his sponge technique in making a rubbing, believed could be read as follows:

OROIT DO RIG FL.ND MA
. . . N . . . O
ROIT DO RIG HERENN OR

which may be translated tentatively as

A prayer for king Fl.nd (son of?)
. . . . . . . . . . . . . . . .
pray for the king of Ireland.

This would seem to suggest that the cross was erected by the king Flann (or Fland) Sinna, who reigned from 879 until 916. The biblical panels on the shaft above the inscription may be identified as follows:

1. *Christ under the tomb-slab,* on which soldiers and others (including Adam's soul?) sit, as a bird breathes into Christ's mouth, suggesting that the moment of Resurrection is at hand.
2. *The Flagellation* (or *Mocking*) *of Christ.*

3. *The soldiers decide not to divide Christ's seamless garment,* and cast lots for it instead. The two flanking soldiers hold the T-shaped garment in front of the central soldier who holds, but does not use, the cutting knife.

### Head

At the centre is *The Crucifixion* with *Stephaton* and *Longinus,* but the figures at the end of the arms cannot be identified satisfactorily (the elements *Earth* and *Ocean* or, perhaps, *Synagoga* and *Ecclesia* respectively?).

## North side

### Base

On the lower register there are fabulous animals including, apparently, a unicorn, while the upper register bears griffins seemingly trampling something (a human body?) underfoot. These fabulous animals doubtless had a symbolic significance, the griffin – having the head of the eagle, the Lord of the Skies, and the body of a lion, the Lord of the Earth – perhaps referring to Christ as Lord of Heaven and Earth.

### Shaft

Above an ornamental panel there are three enigmatic scenes which may conceivably be related to the desert hermits *Paul and Anthony*. However, the top panel may represent a seated evangelist beneath an Old Testament prophet.

* * *

The main theme of this fascinating cross is the Passion, Death and Resurrection of Christ. The Passion is introduced on the base of the west face with *Christ's entry into Jerusalem,* and continues with *The Flagellation* (or *First Mocking*?) before the eye rises to *The Crucifixion* at the centre of the head, while the south side of the base bears an 'overflow' from the face in the form of *The Kiss of Judas*. The bird in the scene of *Christ in the Tomb* at the bottom of the west face of the shaft suggests that the moment of Resurrection is at hand. Probably to be understood as pre-figuring this mystical moment are the two Old Testament panels on the east face (if correctly identified here): Joseph's interpretation of the Butler's dream is that three days later he will be restored to his stewardship, while the scene above shows the fulfilment of this prediction, in the same way that Christ had foretold that he would rise again on the third day. This panel of *Christ in the Tomb* was placed out of its correct chronological order on the shaft so that those kneeling in veneration before the cross would come face to face with a representation of *Christ's Resurrection*. The Resurrection itself, and the associated scene of *The Holy Women coming to the*

*Tomb,* is found on the bottom register of the west face of the base. Above it is *The Raised Christ,* a symbolic representation of Christ as Lord of the Cosmos – an idea probably supported by the symbolism of the griffins around the corner, mentioned above. The culmination of all of these scenes is *The Last Judgment,* with Christ seated in glory above. One further theme present on the cross is that of the Church, perhaps represented by *Ecclesia* on the arm of the west face. *The soldiers casting lots for Christ's seamless garment,* leaving it entire rather than dividing it up among themselves, symbolises the unity of the Church, and related to it is the *Traditio Clavium* scene back to back with it, where Christ hands the heritage of his church to Paul in the form of the Book of the New Testament, and the promise of heaven through the key which he hands to St Peter, giving him the power to bind and loose.

### SOUTH CROSS

Continuing along the gallery of the Interpretative Centre, we come to the South Cross, 3.75 m high, which is approached from its southern side. Before being brought inside in 1993, it stood close to the west door of Temple Doolin, the church beside the Cathedral, where a copy stands today. The south face of the base – the one first encountered by the visitor – bears what is probably an *Adam and Eve* scene, and another which might conceivably represent *The Sacrifice of Isaac.* There are hunting and animal scenes on the east and west faces of the base respectively. The only biblical scene on the cross itself is *The Crucifixion,* which is placed high up on the shaft of the west face. The two figures above Christ's arms may represent *Tellus,* the personification of *Ocean,* on the left, and *Gaia,* personifying the *Earth,* on the right. Two probable features of this representation are unique on Crucifixion scenes on Irish High Crosses. The first is the apparent shield held by Longinus, who pierces Christ's left side, and there- fore, his heart. The second is the blood which pours in three spurts from the wound on to the eyes of Longinus who, according to an old tradition, was thereby cured of his blindness. In a small panel at the bottom of the shaft beneath *The Crucifixion* is a much-abraded and scarcely visible inscription partially deciphered by Dómhnall Ó Murchadha, which could suggest that the cross was erected by the king Maelsechnaill, who reigned from 846 to 862.

### NORTH CROSS

The final round room of the Interpretative Centre houses the fragmentary North Cross which was removed here in 1993 from its open-air location outside the north doorway of the Cathedral. When excavated by Heather King, its base proved to be an old mill-wheel, indicating that it was originally erected at some other location on the site, but where exactly no one can say. What survives of the cross is an almost square-sectioned shaft, the back of which is smooth. The west face is the one first seen by the approaching visitor, and it is divided into square panels of interlace. On the side around the corner to the right is a human figure sitting with crossed legs in a buddha-like pose, while high up on the side back-to-back with it is the tattooed torso and legs of a person entwined by a snake, placed above two biting animals.

Other cross fragments, one bearing a rider, are preserved in the Interpretative Centre, while a further fragment from Clonmacnois is preserved in the National Museum in Dublin.

## Colpe, Co. Meath          See map pages 110-11, square E6
4 KM EAST-SOUTH-EAST OF DROGHEDA; O.S. ½" MAP 13.0-127.744

A small sandstone cross-head preserved in the Church of Ireland church at Colpe was discovered around 1981, and bears a *Crucifixion* on one face.

## Connor, Co. Antrim          See map pages 110-11, square B7
7.5 KM SOUTH-EAST OF BALLYMENA; O.S. ½" MAP 5.J-150.969

The fragmentary shaft of a once fine sandstone cross, now preserved to a height of 1.25 m in the basement of the rectory at Connor, was presumably associated with the monastery founded there in the sixth century, and elevated to Cathedral status in the twelfth century.
One face bears two figured panels:
1. *Cain slays Abel,* with *The Lord* probably being the third figure.
2. A scene (unique on the Irish crosses) of *Joseph being taken out of the pit by his brothers*.

There may be a possible *Sacrifice of Isaac* on the bottom of one of the narrow sides, but the remainder of the cross no longer bears traces of figure sculpture, though it doubtless once did so.

## Donaghmore, Co. Down          See map pages 110-11, square C6
8.5 KM NORTH-NORTH-EAST OF NEWRY;
O.S. ½" MAP 9.J-104.349

The only remnant of the early monastery founded here by St MacErc around the middle of the fifth century is a granite

High Cross, now standing to the south of the modern church. It consists of a shaft and head which did not belong together originally. The two fragments, totalling 2.85 m in height, are, nevertheless, treated together here.

### East face

*Shaft*

It is difficult to identify many of the figures, particularly those grouped in threes, which are piled one on top of the other without any formal division. It is only those around the middle of the shaft and somewhat above it which may be identified with some success. Here we can see two dots-in-circles at a diagonal, representing the sources of the water which *Moses,* lower down to the right, strikes from the rock, as some Israelites drink beneath the water-flow. Above this, to the left, is *David carrying the head of Goliath* on a pole while, further to the right, we find presumably *David slaying the lion.*

*Head*

Though much abraded, the carving probably represents *The Last Judgment.*

Donaghmore, Co. Down-
West face

### South side

The panel on the bottom of the south side of the shaft cannot be identified satisfactorily.

### West face

*Shaft*

1. *Adam and Eve.*
2. *Noah's Ark.*
3. Two unidentified figures.
4. Two figures (one bearing a sword) beneath a horizontal animal.

*Head*

*The Crucifixion,* with a thief on the end of each arm. Unsatisfactorily explained is the presence of one figure between Christ's left hand and the thief, and the two figures between his right hand and the other thief (*Ocean* and *Earth* respectively?).

### North side

(?) *David and Goliath.*

\* \* \*

The choice of scenes on the shaft, and the prevalence of Old Testament material, is typical of the northern crosses. *Moses smiting water from the rock* and *David with the head of Goliath* seem to link this cross with the iconography of the Monasterboice crosses (pages 85ff).

## Donaghmore, Co. Meath

SEE UNDER DUBLIN – NATIONAL MUSEUM (PAGE 52)

## Donaghmore, Co. Tyrone    See map pages 110-11, square C6

3 KM NORTH-WEST OF DUNGANNON;
O.S. ½" MAP 4.H-768.654

The village of Donaghmore in Co. Tyrone marks the site of a monastery which St Patrick founded for St Columb in the fifth century. The focal point of the village is the sandstone High Cross, consisting of a head and a shaft from two separate crosses, which were mounted one on top of the other in 1776 to a height of 3.88 m. The two fragments are treated together here.

**East face** (straight ahead as you come up the village street)

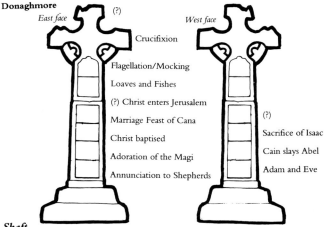

Donaghmore

East face    (?)

West face

Crucifixion

Flagellation/Mocking

Loaves and Fishes

(?) Christ enters Jerusalem

Marriage Feast of Cana

Christ baptised

Adoration of the Magi

Annunciation to Shepherds

(?)

Sacrifice of Isaac

Cain slays Abel

Adam and Eve

*Shaft*

1. *An angel announces the birth of Jesus* to a shepherd across three of the latter's animals.
2. *Adoration of the Magi,* with the Virgin seated second from the left, holding the Christ child horizontally on her lap as she is approached by the three Magi. There is a star on each side of the Virgin's head.
3. *The Baptism of Christ* in the waters of the Jordan which lap around his feet, as the dove descends upon his head.

45

4. *The Marriage Feast of Cana*.
5. The bottom of a further, much-damaged, panel which may show the legs of the pony on which *Christ rides into Jerusalem* at the beginning of his Passion.

### Head

On the shaft beneath the ring are *The Multiplication of the Loaves and Fishes* and *The Flagellation* (or *Mocking*) *of Christ*. At the centre of the head is *The Crucifixion,* with angels flying towards Christ's head. The figures on the arms probably

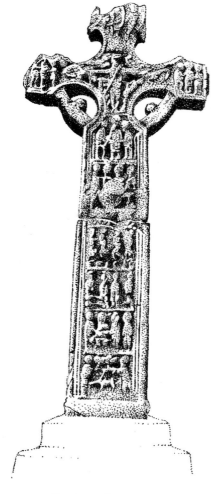

*Donaghmore, Co. Tyrone - East face*

represent the thieves being beaten by soldiers, but the figures above Christ's head are too worn to be identified satisfactorily.

**South side**

The hemisphere at the bottom of the shaft may contain the arched body of *the wolf suckling Romulus and Remus,* the founders of Rome.

**West face**

Unusually for the northern crosses, there is a horseman on the base and a possible animal procession on the step above it.

*Shaft*
1. *Adam and Eve knowing their nakedness.*
2. *Cain slaying Abel,* with the third figure perhaps representing *The Lord admonishing Cain.*
3. *The Sacrifice of Isaac.*
4. The sculpture is too worn to allow satisfactory identification.

The head shows no biblical scenes.

**North side**

The north side is decorated with a variety of ornamental and animal motifs.

★ ★ ★

The iconography of the shaft fragment corresponds closely to that in Armagh Cathedral (page 20). But it is the cross at Arboe, in the same county (page 16), which not only shares most of its subject-matter, but also gives us the best idea of which scenes are likely to have been present on the head that must once have been mounted on the shaft.

## Downpatrick, Co. Down      See map pages 110-11, square C7
CLOSE TO THE TOWN CENTRE; O.S. ½" MAP 9.J-483.445

The church at Down is traditionally taken to have been founded by St Patrick, whose name only became attached to it after the alleged discovery of his remains there in the twelfth century. His foundation is marked today by the thirteenth-century Protestant Cathedral which was much re-modelled some two centuries ago. It is in and around this Cathedral that we find a number of High Cross fragments.

**CROSS STANDING OUTSIDE THE EAST END OF THE CATHEDRAL**

The figure sculpture on this granite cross, 2.38 m tall, is so worn that interpretation is hazardous. However, the east face

– seen by the visitor approaching from the town – may show a highly unusual selection of scenes illustrating *The Early Life of the Virgin Mary,* the lowermost panel perhaps representing *The Angel bringing bread to the Virgin in the temple,* akin to that at Duleek in Co. Meath (pages 53-55). The head bears *The Crucifixion* with thieves.

The west face, which looks towards the Cathedral, is even more worn, and the only scenes which may be identified with some likelihood are a fragmentary *Adam and Eve* at the bottom of the shaft, and a *Last Judgment* on the head.

## CROSS-FRAGMENTS IN THE CATHEDRAL

In the vestibule of the Cathedral there are fragments of two crosses bearing interlace and spiral ornament. Built into a west-facing wall in the south aisle are the heads of two twelfth-century crosses. Each bears a figure in high relief bearing what looks like a reliquary, and perhaps representing *St Patrick.*

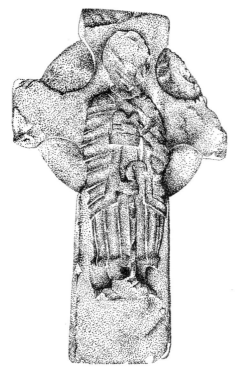

*Downpatrick Cathedral – St. Patrick ?*

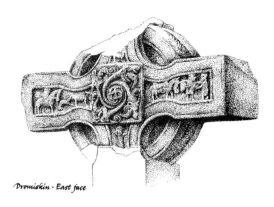

*Dromiskin - East face*

## Dromiskin, Co. Louth

See map pages 110–11, square D6

9.5 KM SOUTH OF DUNDALK; O.S. ½" MAP 13.O-052.982

Mounted on a modern shaft in the churchyard at Dromiskin is the head of a granite cross, but where it was originally erected is not known. On the east face, looking away from the nearby Round Tower, is a square plaque with biting animals uncoiling from bosses – probably copying a bronze original. On the south (left) arm, a horse and a dog hunt a deer. On the other arm is a horse bearing a headless human torso, preceded by a figure probably carrying the decapitated head on his back as he walks towards a man, who stretches his hand forth to receive it. The scene may well represent *David bringing the body and severed head of Goliath to King Saul in Jerusalem,* as found also on the North Cross at Ahenny in Co. Tipperary (page 16). The west face bears an attractively decorated boss at the centre of the head, probably also copied from a bronze original.

## Drumcliff, Co. Sligo

See map pages 110–11, square C4

6.5 KM NORTH-NORTH-WEST OF SLIGO;
O.S. ½" MAP 7.G-681.420

The remains of a monastery founded here in the sixth century by St Colmcille include the stump of a Round Tower on one side of the road, and two sandstone High Crosses standing in a graveyard on the other side, together with fragments of a third now preserved in the National Museum in Dublin (page 52). One of the crosses still *in situ* is located at the narrow end of the graveyard; it is an undecorated shaft, missing its ringed head which vanished centuries ago. The more important cross, 3.83 m high, overlooks the roadway leading to the Church of Ireland church and the grave of W. B. Yeats. The shaft shows signs of having been altered to fit the head which it now bears.

49

**Drumcliff**

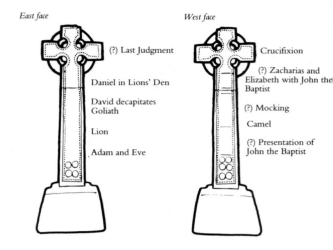

*East face*

(?) Last Judgment

Daniel in Lions' Den

David decapitates Goliath

Lion

Adam and Eve

*West face*

Crucifixion

(?) Zacharias and Elizabeth with John the Baptist

(?) Mocking

Camel

(?) Presentation of John the Baptist

## East face

*Adam and Eve* stand on a circular interlace, as the serpent climbs its way up the apple tree which blossoms above their heads. Further up, *David cuts off the head of Goliath* above a splendidly prancing lion in high relief. At the bottom of the head is *Daniel in the Lions' Den,* while the scene at the centre of the head may represent *The Last Judgment,* or some kindred scene, to which numerous heads belong.

## South side

The shaft bears spiral ornament and animal interlace. There are animals in high relief on the head, and the end of the arm bears the only representation of *The Virgin and Child* known on an Irish High Cross.

## West face

Above an interlace at the bottom of the shaft there are three figures, of which the central one holds a child. While they could be *The Holy Family,* they may well represent *Zacharias and Elizabeth holding the infant John the Baptist* as they present him in the Temple. Above a camel in high relief there is a possible *Mocking of Christ.* The scene at the bottom of the head could be *The Holy Family returning from Egypt,* or, conceivably, *Zacharias and Elizabeth bringing the infant John the Baptist to the Temple* for his circumcision. At the centre of the head is *The Crucifixion.*

*Drumcliff - East face*

## Drumcullin, Co. Offaly

See map pages 110-11, square E5

12.5 KM EAST-NORTH-EAST OF BIRR;
O.S. ½" MAP 15.N-181.061

Close to an old church on the site of a sixth-century monastery is the head of a sandstone cross bearing *The Crucifixion* on one face. The other face bears spiral and interlace ornament.

## Dublin – The National Museum of Ireland

See map pages 110-11, square E6/7

IN THE CITY CENTRE; O.S. ½" MAP 13.O-162.338

The National Museum in Dublin houses a number of High Cross fragments. The only one currently on display is a fine decorated pillar from Banagher, Co. Offaly, showing a horseman, a lion, a deer in a trap and a human interlace on one face, and the other has the upper part of two human bodies growing out of an interlace, as well as a lion and an interlace. The scenes on two fragments from Drumcliff, Co. Sligo, include *The Sacrifice of Isaac, Daniel in the Lions' Den, Christ, The Resurrection* and a *Flagellation* or *Mocking of Christ*. A cross-head from Durrow, Co. Offaly has *The Crucifixion* on one face and a probable *David as Shepherd* on the other. Other fragments come from Clonmacnois, Co. Offaly, Balsitric, Co. Dublin, Inishcealtra, Co. Clare, Monasterboice, Co. Louth, Killary, Co. Meath and probably Donaghmore, Co. Meath.

*Banagher slab in the National Museum, Dublin*

*Duleek - East face*

## Duleek, Co. Meath

See map pages 110-11, square E6

8 KM SOUTH-WEST OF DROGHEDA; O.S. ½" MAP 13.O-046.684

Standing between the road and the disused Church of
Ireland church near the centre of the village is one of the
smallest of the sandstone Irish High Crosses, being only
1.82 m high. The figure sculpture, confined to the west face,
is unusual in that it seems to illustrate scenes from *The early
life of the Virgin* as found in the apocryphal Gospel of James,
known as the Proto-Evangelium, which may also be present
on the cross at Downpatrick, Co. Down (page 48). They
may be identified tentatively as:

Duleek - West face

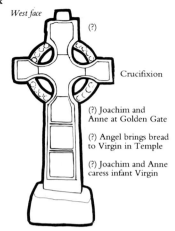

**Duleek**

*West face*

(?)

Crucifixion

(?) Joachim and
Anne at Golden Gate

(?) Angel brings bread
to Virgin in Temple

(?) Joachim and Anne
caress infant Virgin

1. *Joachim and Anne caressing the infant Virgin.*
2. *An angel brings bread to the Virgin in the Temple.*
3. *Joachim and Anne greet one another at the Golden Gate.*

If these interpretations be correct, the scenes are not in their correct order, which should be 3.1.2. *The Crucifixion* is the only scene on the head which can be reliably identified. The other face and the two sides of the cross bear interesting combinations of geometrical ornament and fabulous beasts, whose symbolic significance is now lost to us.

On the other side of the church is a cross-head with *The Crucifixion* on one face, the other bearing no figures.

## Durrow, Co. Offaly
See map pages 110-11, square E5
6 KM NORTH-NORTH-WEST OF TULLAMORE;
O.S. ½" MAP 15.N-320.307

The Columban monastery at Durrow, from whence came the famous book of the name now in the Library of Trinity College in Dublin, has one well-preserved sandstone High Cross *in situ,* standing to a height of 3.74 m. The head of a second cross was brought to the National Museum in Dublin (page 52) in 1992.

**East face** (looking towards the entrance to the graveyard from the road)
1. *The Raised Christ,* where Christ, flanked on each side by an angel, is literally raised above two apostles, Peter and Paul. He places his feet on their knees as they hold a book open in front of him.
2. A panel of four interlace knots.
3. *The Sacrifice of Isaac.*

*Durrow - Head of East face*

The centre of the head shows Christ bearing the sceptre and cross-staff normally associated with *The Last Judgment*, though the good and bad souls which normally accompany the scene are absent. But *the piper* and *David with his harp* on one side of Christ do form part of the Last Judgment on Muiredach's Cross at Monasterboice, Co. Louth (page 88). On the other side of Christ are a lamb, and *David (or Samson?) slaying the lion*.

### South side

The three scenes on the shaft represent *Eve giving the apple to Adam*, *Cain slaying Abel* and *David as king*. On the head, the underside of the ring is decorated with three human heads

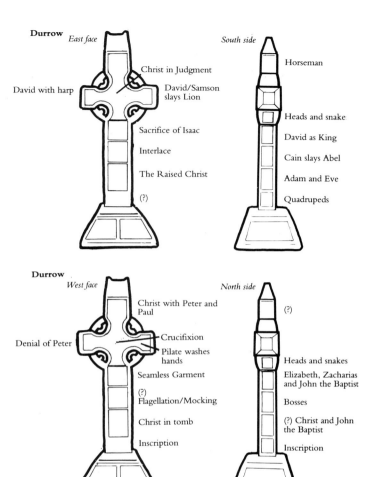

Durrow — East face

- Christ in Judgment
- David/Samson slays Lion
- David with harp
- Sacrifice of Isaac
- Interlace
- The Raised Christ
- (?)

South side

- Horseman
- Heads and snake
- David as King
- Cain slays Abel
- Adam and Eve
- Quadrupeds

Durrow — West face

- Christ with Peter and Paul
- Crucifixion
- Pilate washes hands
- Denial of Peter
- Seamless Garment
- (?)
- Flagellation/Mocking
- Christ in tomb
- Inscription

North side

- (?)
- Heads and snakes
- Elizabeth, Zacharias and John the Baptist
- Bosses
- (?) Christ and John the Baptist
- Inscription

enmeshed by a snake, probably representing the evil which Christ overcame at the Crucifixion. On top is a horseman (apocalyptic?).

**West face**

Above an imperfect inscription (with the surviving letters DUBT) at the bottom of the shaft, there are three biblical panels.

1. *Christ in the Tomb,* with a bird breathing life into the body of Christ beneath the stone on which the soldiers sleep.
2. *The Flagellation* (or *First Mocking?) of Christ.*
3. *The soldiers with Christ's seamless garment.*

Flanking *The Crucifixion* at the centre of the head is *The*

*Denial of Peter* on the left arm, and *Pilate washing his hands* on the right. The uppermost panel is the *Traditio Clavium,* in which Christ hands the key of the kingdom to St Peter and the Book of the New Testament to St Paul.

**North side**
A panel at the bottom of the shaft contains an imperfect inscription which probably proclaimed that the cross was erected by Maelsechnaill, king of Ireland (846–862). The two figured scenes above it are:
1. Two figures apparently embracing one another. As their shoulders are bared, they may well represent *John the Baptist recognising Christ* in the desert.
2. *Elizabeth carrying the infant John the Baptist,* as *Zacharias* holds his hand up to his mouth in a gesture of being dumb, which he was until he wrote the name of his son John on a tablet (Luke i, 63–64). The figure at the top of the cross has not been identified.

★ ★ ★

This cross shares many subjects and themes with the Cross of the Scriptures at Clonmacnois, Co. Offaly (page 37), and the panels on the shaft of the west face are virtually identical on both crosses. But the Old Testament scenes of the south side are absent at Clonmacnois, as is also one of the most interesting features of this cross – the apparent emphasis on John the Baptist in the panels on the narrow north side. This characteristic is also echoed on the Tall Cross at Monasterboice, Co. Louth (page 92), and reflects the importance of Baptism, which was the only sacrament other than the Eucharist recognised in the ninth century.

## Dysert O'Dea, Co. Clare See map pages 110-11, square F3

4 KM SOUTH OF COROFIN; O.S. ½" MAP 14.R-281.847

A twelfth-century limestone High Cross stands 3.27 m high in a field to the east of the Romanesque church and Round Tower at Dysert O'Dea. Shaft and head are unlikely to have been designed for one another originally, and both were erected together by Michael O'Dea in 1683, and again by F. H. Synge (a cousin of the playwright) in 1871.

The visitor approaching from the church sees first the west face, which is decorated with cross-shapes and animal interlacings – and, at the centre of the head, what must surely be one of the earliest surviving St Brigid's crosses. The base shows *Adam and Eve* between the broadly-expanding

*Dysert O'Dea - East face*

fruit-laden branches of the apple tree. Around the corner on the base are *Daniel in the Lions' Den* (on the right) and an unidentified scene. The east face of the cross is dominated by a figure of *Christ* (head not original!) dressed in a long robe and triumphantly stretching forth his arms and, beneath him, a bishop with mitre and volute crozier, probably representing the local saint, *Tola,* who founded a monastery here in the eighth century.

## Fahan Mura, Co. Donegal  See map pages 110-11, square A5
5.5 KM SOUTH OF BUNCRANA; O.S. ½" MAP 1.C-345.264

*Fahan Mura - West face of slab*

A ruined church in an old graveyard at Fahan, beside the road from Letterkenny to Buncrana, marks the site of a monastery founded by St Colmcille for his disciple Mura. The 2.10 m tall slab standing close to the church is not a High Cross as such, but is included here because its uneven arm-stumps have been seen by some as evidence for the 'breaking out' of the cross-form from the cross-slab, and thereby marking the first step in the development of the High Cross. If anything, however, the slab demonstrates close connections with Scotland, where the shape is more at home. Approaching from the gate of the churchyard, the visitor sees one face with a decorative cross of interlace at the foot of which stand two unidentified figures bearing undeciphered inscriptions on their cloaks. Back-to-back with it is another interlaced cross of a different shape. What makes this cross-slab unique in Ireland, however, is the presence of a Greek inscription on one narrow side which may be translated as 'Glory and honour to the Father and the Son and to the Holy Ghost' – a doxology approved by the Council of Toledo in 633.

## (Fennor), Slane, Co. Meath   See map pages 110-11, square E6
IN THE TOWN OF SLANE; O.S. ½" MAP 13.N-965.745

A cross-head of sandstone which was found in 1990 in the churchyard at Fennor – near the south bank of the Boyne – is now displayed in the Catholic church at Slane. It bears a *Crucifixion* on one face, with some unidentified figures above and below.

## Galloon, Co. Fermanagh   See map pages 110-11, square C5
4.5 KM SOUTH-WEST OF NEWTOWNBUTLER;
O.S. ½" MAP 8.H-391.227

The peaceful, old graveyard at Galloon, attractively sited close to a lake, housed four High Crosses. One fragmentary cross was stolen more than twenty years ago; another was removed to safety by the Department of the Environment, and two sandstone shaft fragments still remain on site.

### EAST CROSS, LOCATED CLOSE TO THE GATE OF THE GRAVEYARD
The west face, with its back to the hedge, bears in ascending order, *The Adoration of the Magi, John the Baptist baptising Christ in the Jordan,* and *The raven brings bread to the desert*

**Galloon – East Cross**

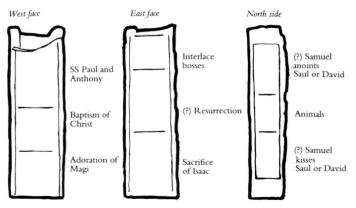

| West face | East face | North side |
|---|---|---|
| SS Paul and Anthony | Interlace bosses | (?) Samuel anoints Saul or David |
| Baptism of Christ | (?) Resurrection | Animals |
| Adoration of Magi | Sacrifice of Isaac | (?) Samuel kisses Saul or David |

*hermits Paul and Anthony*. The other face, best seen through the hedge, shows *The Sacrifice of Isaac* below and a probable, if unusual, *Resurrection* above. One of the narrow sides has two embracing figures (perhaps *Samuel kissing Saul* or *David*) and, above two animals, *Samuel anointing Saul* or *David*.

## WEST CROSS, AT THE TOP OF THE SLOPING GRAVEYARD

The east face, looking out over the graveyard, should – unusually – be read from top to bottom as follows: *Adam and Eve, Daniel in the Lions' Den* and, on the bottom, perhaps a *Baptism* scene, with John the Baptist on the left, Christ in the centre, and a smaller, wingless angel-figure on the right. Back-to-back with it on the west face are three panels, again to be read from top to bottom as follows: a much-abraded *Noah's Ark, The Sacrifice of Isaac,* and an angel spreading its wings to protect the *Three Children in the Fiery Furnace*.

# Glendalough, Co. Wicklow   See map pages 110-11, square F6
19 KM WEST-NORTH-WEST OF WICKLOW;
O.S. ½" MAP 16.T-121.968

'The Valley of the two lakes', where St Kevin founded a monastery in the sixth/seventh century, has a number of crosses scattered over a variety of locations, but the only one

*Glendalough, Market Cross*

62

to bear figure sculpture is the Market Cross, now in the Interpretative Centre, where a number of other crosses are also stored. On one face of the Market Cross, *the crucified Christ* is carved in high relief on the head, above the figure of a bishop or abbot, probably representing the founding saint, *Kevin*. There are two further figures on the base.

## Graiguenamanagh, Co. Kilkenny

See map pages 110–11, square G5–6

IN TOWN CENTRE; O.S. ½" MAP 19.S-719.768

In the grounds of the parish church (formerly the Cistercian abbey of Duiske) at Graiguenamanagh, there are two granite crosses, both of which were brought here from other sites in the locality.

### NORTH CROSS (ORIGINALLY FROM BALLYOGAN)
Standing on a base decorated with a ringed cross and geometrical motifs, the shaft of the east face bears *David playing his harp, The Sacrifice of Isaac,* and *Adam and Eve* (or *The Lord reproving Adam*), above which is *The Crucifixion* on the head of the cross.

The west face is largely occupied by S-spirals. Beneath them is *The Visitation*, with the Virgin embracing Elizabeth

*Graiguenamanagh North Cross- West face*

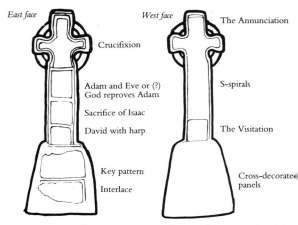

*East face*

Crucifixion

Adam and Eve or (?)
God reproves Adam

Sacrifice of Isaac

David with harp

Key pattern

Interlace

*West face*

The Annunciation

S-spirals

The Visitation

Cross-decorated
panels

in the presence of a servant, and at the top is *The Annunciation,* with the Virgin seated on the right being approached from the left by an angel. This is the only instance of these two scenes on the Irish crosses.

## SOUTH CROSS (ORIGINALLY FROM AGHAILTA)
Standing close by is a rather degenerate cross showing unusually *The Crucifixion* on both faces.

## Inishcealtra, Co. Clare
See map pages 110–11, square F4
5.5 KM EAST-NORTH-EAST OF SCARRIFF;
O.S. ½" MAP 15.R-698.849

The island monastery of Inishcealtra in Lough Derg, on the river Shannon, preserves a Round Tower and a number of churches which probably served pilgrims who flocked here down to the seventeenth century. Among the other monuments on the island are a number of sandstone crosses, most of which have been placed against the interior walls of the Romanesque St Caimin's Church. One of these, 1.60 m high, bears a curious animal holding a human leg in its mouth on a panel at the foot of the cross. The west side bears an inscription asking for a prayer for the Chief Elder of Ireland, Cathasach, while the east side bears another inscription asking for a prayer for Tornoc (or Turlough?) who erected the cross. As Cathasach died in 1111, the cross was probably erected some years earlier.

Attached to the north wall of the church is the head of another cross which has damaged figures on the ends of the arms. By comparison with the East Cross at Galloon, Co. Fermanagh (page 61), these may be tentatively identified as

*Samuel kissing and anointing Saul* or *David*. The Romanesque head of a *Christ* figure, probably part of a Crucifixion from a twelfth-century cross, was discovered by Liam de Paor during his excavation more than twenty years ago, but it has since been deposited in the National Museum in Dublin.

## Kells, Co. Meath See map pages 110-11, square D6

IN THE TOWN CENTRE; O.S. ½" MAP 13.N.739-740.759

Kells is one of the most important, in fact probably *the* most important, High Cross site in the country, where the series of Irish Scripture Crosses may well have been initiated. In addition to a Round Tower and St Columb's House surviving from the monastery founded by monks from Iona in the early ninth century, there are remains of four sandstone High Crosses – two virtually complete, one incomplete and one unfinished – as well as a decorated cross-base which lies close to the tall square tower near the Church of Ireland church.

### BROKEN CROSS

The Broken Cross, 3.44 m high, is a cross-shaft standing about 50 m away from the west door of the Protestant church, now probably occupying the site of the major church of the monastery. To judge by its present incomplete state, this cross must once have been one of the finest and most impressive of all the Irish High Crosses, and the disappearance of its head – which may well lie buried somewhere nearby – must surely be accounted one of the saddest losses among High Crosses. The cross may not always have stood exactly where it now stands, however, because the fact that the Old Testament face (which normally looks towards the east) actually faces west suggests that the shaft has been re-erected at some period unknown. The narrow sides are richly decorated with a variety of geometrical and interlacing devices, and the figure sculpture is confined to the two main faces. The base bears only mouldings.

**East face** (looking towards the church)
The six rectangular panels may be identified tentatively as follows:

1. *The Baptism of Christ*.
2. *The Marriage Feast of Cana*.
3. Apparently two separate scenes, probably representing (a) on the left, *Christ raises his hand to the lame man* with his bed on his back, as the angel (beneath Christ) flies down towards the bottom left-hand corner to trouble the waters *at the pool of Bethesda* and (b) on the right,

65

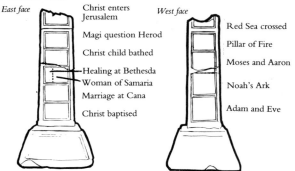

*East face*

Christ enters Jerusalem

Magi question Herod

Christ child bathed

Healing at Bethesda
Woman of Samaria
Marriage at Cana

Christ baptised

*West face*

Red Sea crossed

Pillar of Fire

Moses and Aaron

Noah's Ark

Adam and Eve

the seated *Christ, raising his hand to the woman of Samaria* (who may clasp a water jar), accompanied by a disciple.

4. *The Christ child being washed in a tub,* with water poured in by the two mid-wives present at his birth according to apocryphal sources, the believing Zelome on the right and Salome on the left, behind whom is perhaps an angel. Salome at first doubted the virgin birth, whereupon her hand withered; but after an angel had told her that the Lord had hearkened unto her, her hand was healed when she approached the Christ child.

5. *The Three Wise Men,* or Magi, *approach* from the right towards *Herod* (guarded by two bowmen) *to ask him where the Christ child was.*

6. *The Entry of Christ into Jerusalem* (fragmentary).

**West face** (with its back to the church)

Unlike the east face, there are only five panels on this face,

*Adam and Eve on the west face of the Broken Cross at Kells*

66

the two lower ones being larger and almost square in shape, while the upper ones are rectangular, as on the other face.

1. A charming *Adam and Eve*.
2. *Noah's Ark,* with the head and feet of God behind it on the right, and the heads of those drowned in the Flood beneath the hull on the left.
3. On the left, *Moses and Aaron,* the latter raising his rod to *change the waters of Egypt into blood,* as Pharaoh with his guard (on the right) looks on in horror, in the presence of two of his servants (below).
4. *The Pillar with the fire* on top, leading the praying Israelites, who flank it, back to the promised land.
5. The only surviving part of the panel shows the rippling waters of the Red Sea, in which the legs of the Egyptians and their floundering horses can be seen, as the (no longer surviving) *Israelites find their passage safely to the other side of the Red Sea.*

★ ★ ★

This cross, which may have been one of the earliest of the Scripture series, merits a lengthier discussion here because it shows us how a particular theme was illustrated through a choice of highly unusual scenes, and also how one face can be seen to inter-relate with the other back-to-back with it. If the identifications given above be correct, this cross has seven out of a total of twelve scenes which are found on no other cross. This is partially explained by the fact that a number of the scenes were chosen specifically to illustrate a single theme – the cleansing power of water in the sacrament of baptism. Noah was saved in water and the Israelites passed unharmed through the Red Sea, whereas others perished. Although the washing of the Christ child is not described in the Gospels (nor even in the apocrypha), it is the first cleansing of Christ by water, the second being the baptism in the Jordan. At Cana, Christ used water for his first miracle, changing it into wine, both of which are used in the Eucharist, instituted at The Last Supper (which may have been illustrated on the lost cross-head). The lame man was healed by Christ at the pool of Bethesda, and the Saviour's words to the Samaritan woman at the well, 'the water that I shall give . . . shall be . . . a well of water springing up into everlasting life' (John iv, 14) have been construed in connection with baptism. Baptism is, indeed, the central theme of this cross, and the placing of the Baptism scene out of its proper chronological order on the bottom of the New Testament face (unlike the other face which places the Old Testament panels in their correct biblical order) was doubtless designed to allow the faithful to see it in front of them as they knelt before the cross. It was not until the twelfth century that the number of sacraments were codified as seven and, in the ninth century, Baptism and the Eucharist were seen as the only two sacraments of the church by Paschasius Radbertus, whose work on 'The Body and Blood of Christ' (831-833) finds a visual illustration on this cross.

Another reason for the unusually high number of scenes occurring only on this cross is that some of them were selected to facilitate the correlation of the Old and New Testament scenes on each face. This can be seen particularly in the uppermost panels where, for instance, the common denominator of the horse/pony brings the Israelites to safety through the Red Sea and carries Christ to his Passion, Death and Resurrection in Jerusalem. An analogous concordance can be found in the corresponding two panels beneath these: The Pillar of Fire and the star which led the Magi to Herod each represent a supernatural light which guided the good towards the promised Lord. Moses (and Aaron) changing the waters of Egypt into Blood pre-figures the change from water into wine at the marriage feast of Cana – and the transformation of the wine into the Blood of Christ at the consecration of the mass. Adam and Eve on the bottom of the Old Testament face are the first human generation, and back-to-back with them on the New Testament face is The Baptism, which is to be understood as a re-generation of mankind. In short, even in its truncated state, this cross offers the most fascinating collection and selection of biblical scenes on any of the Irish crosses, and demonstrates the careful planning which went into the design of these great monuments.

## MARKET CROSS

It is only within the last century that this name has been applied to the cross which stands 3.35 m high at one of the most important road junctions in the centre of the town of Kells – in constant danger of being shattered by an errant juggernaut. As the inscription on the bottom of the north face of the shaft reminds us, it was re-erected in 1688, at a time when the Catholic population was anticipating a more liberal attitude under the new king James II – but in vain, as James was deposed only two years later by William of Orange. Wherever it stood originally, the main faces would almost certainly have been orientated east-west, but the existing directions are retained here for convenience.

**East side** (looking down John street)
Most of the scenes on this side are very enigmatic, starting

with the base where two centaurs (one with a bow, the other with a trident) move leftwards towards two birds facing one another, one standing on a fish, the other on a quadruped. None of the panels of the shaft can be identified satisfactorily, though the lower three may derive from a cycle in the life of either *St Peter* or *St John the Baptist,* with the third panel up possibly representing the saint in prison. Even more problematical is the uppermost panel, showing a horned creature (devil?) flanked by two upright quadrupeds. The only identifiable scene is on the end of the arm, where we find *the raven bringing bread to the hermits Paul and Anthony in the desert.*

**South face** (looking towards Cross Street)

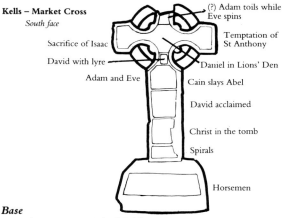

Kells – **Market Cross**
*South face*

(?) Adam toils while Eve spins

Temptation of St Anthony

Sacrifice of Isaac

Daniel in Lions' Den

David with lyre

Cain slays Abel

Adam and Eve

David acclaimed

Christ in the tomb

Spirals

Horsemen

*Base*
Four horsemen with shields.

*Shaft*
1. *Christ in the Tomb,* guarded by soldiers.
2. *David (acclaimed king),* with his army of Israelites.
3. Left, *Adam and Eve knowing their nakedness.* Right, *Cain slaying Abel.*

At the centre of the head is *Daniel in the Lions' Den.* Beneath him, *David plays his lyre* and, above him, perhaps *Adam and Eve holding one of their children* ('Adam toils while Eve spins'). On the left arm is *The Sacrifice of Isaac* (with a chalice-like object in the contraction of the arm), while on the right arm is *The Temptation of St Anthony* (with two contorting animals in the contraction).

**West side** (facing Market Street)
On the base are soldiers with spears and shields fighting others with swords and shields.

*Kells, Market Cross - South face*

**Kells – Market Cross**

*West side*

David slays the Lion

Hand of God shows Moses and the Israelites the way through the desert

Judgment of Solomon or (?) Massacre of the Innocents

(?) David charges Solomon or Samuel anoints David

Man spearing stag

Soldiers fighting

*Shaft*

1. A man spearing a stag (significance unknown).
2. Two soldiers holding a figure upside down – part of a *Judgment of Solomon* scene? Or, less likely, *The Massacre of the Innocents*.
3. *David's charge to Solomon,* or (?) *Samuel anoints David*.
4. *The Hand of God shows Moses* (left) *and the Israelites* (below) *the way through the desert*.

On the end of the arm is *David slaying the lion*.

**North face** (looking towards Castle Street)

On the base, a man hunts or herds animals towards the left.

*Shaft*

1. The bottom panel was chiselled away to make way for an inscription proclàiming that Robert Balfe of

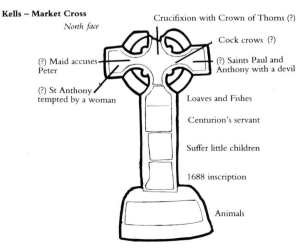

**Kells – Market Cross**

*North face*

Crucifixion with Crown of Thorns (?)

Cock crows (?)

(?) Maid accuses Peter

(?) Saints Paul and Anthony with a devil

(?) St Anthony tempted by a woman

Loaves and Fishes

Centurion's servant

Suffer little children

1688 inscription

Animals

Galmorestown, sovereign of the corporation of Kells, re-erected the cross in 1688.

2. The seated *Christ* (damaged, on the left) *suffering the little children to come unto him*.

3. Above crouching figures of unknown significance, *Christ heals the centurion's servant,* with the centurion kneeling and his servant diagonally above his back.

4. *The Miracle of the Loaves and Fishes.*

### Head

At the centre of the head is *The Crucifixion,* with what appears to be one of the earliest known examples of the Crown of Thorns above his head. Beneath him is a crouching figure with a water jar (*Tellus / Ocean,* or possibly even one of the *Holy Women bringing a jar of ointment to the Tomb?*). Flanking Christ's left hand is a scarcely visible cock, and flanking his right a small figure (both belonging to a *Denial of Peter* scene?). On the left arm is a figure, perhaps St *Anthony,* jabbing his tau- (or T-) shaped crozier into the foot of a woman (the hermit overcoming the devil in the guise of a woman?), while the right arm probably represents *Saints Paul and Anthony fighting the devil* (upside down).

* * *

This cross has a number of unusual representations and features, including the possible scenes from the life of *St Peter* or *John the Baptist* on the east side, the three miracles on the north side of the shaft (the inscription probably replaced a fourth), and *Daniel* featuring prominently at the centre of the head of the south face, in a pose pre-figuring *The Crucifixion* back-to-back with it. But what is perhaps the most unusual feature of all – if the identifications proposed here be correct – is the frieze of subjects at arm level illustrating events in the life of the desert hermits *Paul and Anthony,* in their efforts to overcome evil. These represent perhaps the greatest number of scenes from a Paul and Anthony cycle to survive anywhere on a single monument of the first millennium.

### THE CROSS OF SAINTS PATRICK AND COLUMBA

Standing close to and, at mid-morning, literally in the shadow of the Round Tower of the old Columban monastery, is the Cross of Saints Patrick and Columba, 3.30 m high, which gets its name from an inscription proclaiming that this is the cross of Saints Patrick and Columba. This inscription which, unusually for the Irish crosses, is in Latin and on the base, may perhaps document a coalescing of two rival groupings which had been fighting for power and

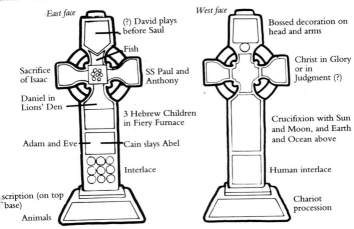

*East face* — (?) David plays before Saul; Fish; SS Paul and Anthony; Sacrifice of Isaac; Daniel in Lions' Den; 3 Hebrew Children in Fiery Furnace; Adam and Eve; Cain slays Abel; Interlace; Inscription (on top of base); Animals

*West face* — Bossed decoration on head and arms; Christ in Glory or in Judgment (?); Crucifixion with Sun and Moon, and Earth and Ocean above; Human interlace; Chariot procession

possessions since the seventh century – the Patrician *paruchia,* or family of churches or monasteries, based in Armagh, and the Columban *paruchia* centred in Iona, but which had expanded to Kells a number of decades before the cross was erected. The panels of this cross seem less disciplined yet demonstrate a greater freedom in design by not having its biblical panels formally separated by frames, instead of which they are either kept apart by interlace or are simply juxtaposed above or beside one another.

**East face** (looking obliquely towards the Round Tower)
On the base, a man hunts animals, while on its upper surface is the inscription referred to above:

PATRICII ET COLUMBAE CRUX
The Cross of Patrick and Columba.

Above an interlace on the bottom of the shaft is a panel conflating *Adam and Eve* and *Cain slaying Abel,* as on the present south face of the Market Cross in the town. Just above it, an angel spreads its wings to protect *The Three Hebrew Children in the Fiery Furnace,* its flames fuelled by soldiers bringing faggots right and left. The bottom of the head is occupied by *Daniel in the Lions' Den,* and above his head is a nest of bosses in a square bed of interlace. On the left arm is *The Sacrifice of Isaac* and, on the right arm, *the raven brings bread to the desert hermits Paul and Anthony.* In the upper limb are two crossed fish, above which *David plays his harp,* probably before Saul on the right – the coil behind the latter's ear possibly representing the evil which David banished with his playing.

73

*Kells, Cross of SS. Patrick and Columba - East face*

**South side** (facing the Round Tower)

The only biblical subject here is *David slaying the lion* on the end of the arm, though a quadruped can be seen attacking a centaur at the top of the head.

**West face** (with its back to the Round Tower)

On the base, a chariot with rider and charioteer proceed towards the left, preceded by two horsemen. Above a human interlace at the bottom of the shaft is *The Crucifixion* with an eagle (of Resurrection?) on Christ's head. Above his arms are two figures, representing perhaps *Ocean* (on the left) and *Earth,* above which appear the *Sun* and *Moon* which, taken all together, comprise four elements which give a cosmic symbolism to Christ's death on the cross. At the centre of the head is a scene with Christ which has elements of *The Last Judgment* (cross-staff and sceptre) and of the *Christ in Glory* of the Apocalyptic Vision (lamb) without making clear precisely which subject is meant.

**North side**

The identity of the figure on the end of the arm is uncertain. So, too, is that of the two figures on top of the shaft, but as the one seen on the right may hold up a panel bearing a ringed cross, we may have here a representation of the two saints mentioned in the inscription. If so, these would be the earliest surviving representations of either of these two great churchmen.

**UNFINISHED CROSS**

To the south of the Protestant church is an unfinished cross, showing us the rough form of a cross before the final carving was executed. At the centre of the head of the east face (looking towards the town centre) is a *Crucifixion,* with an unusually tall Christ robed to the knees. The figures on the north arm may be *The Holy Women being met by the angel at the Tomb* on Easter Sunday morn. The cross lay in fragments until re-erected in the late nineteenth century.

## Kilfenora, Co. Clare See map pages 110-11, square F3

IN THE TOWN CENTRE; O.S. ½" MAP 14.R-182.940

The twelfth century saw the creation of at least seven limestone High Crosses in Kilfenora, of which one (page 78) was removed to Killaloe in the same county in 1821. Of the remaining six still on the site, only two are fairly complete and bear figure sculpture. One of these is what is known as the Doorty cross which stands 2.83 m high outside the west wall of the Cathedral, and gets its name from a family which used a part of the cross (upside down) as its gravemarker. Most of the sculpture is, to say the least, enigmatic.

The east face (looking towards the Cathedral) is dominated by a bishop or abbot bearing a volute crozier and an old-fashioned mitre, of a kind preserved today only in the papal

*Kilfenora, Doorty Cross - East face*

tiara. He may represent *St Fachtnan,* the founder of the church at Kilfenora. Beneath him, two further figures in high relief (*SS Paul and Anthony*?) plunge the butts of their respective croziers – one of the old Irish drop-headed variety, the other T-shaped – into a winged beast, beneath which are two human heads. Neither of the two figures on the narrow south side are identifiable. On the face with its back to the Cathedral, there is what can only be presumed to be a figure of *the crucified Christ* on the head, and the roof of a shrine(?) with a horseman (pilgrim?) on the shaft.

## WEST CROSS

In a field to the west of the Cathedral is a thin cross, 4.60 m high, on which the figure of *the crucified Christ* – standing on a pedestal and bearing a satchel/reliquary on his breast – is carved in high relief on the east face. The west face bears interlace and geometrical ornament.

*Kilfenora, West Cross –
Head of west face*

## Kilgobbin, Co. Dublin  See map pages 110–11, square E6/7

10 KM SOUTH-EAST OF DUBLIN; O.S. ½" MAP 16.O-190.244

A granite cross at Kilgobbin, on the slopes of the Dublin mountains, tapers downwards; it bears a figure of the *crucified Christ* on one face, and a similar figure (a *Risen Christ?*) on the other.

## Kilkieran, Co. Kilkenny  See map pages 110–11, square G5

4.5 KM NORTH-NORTH-WEST OF CARRICK-ON-SUIR;
O.S. ½" MAP 18.S-422.274

One of the sandstone crosses at Kilkieran, which resembles that at Ahenny not far away, has a series of horsemen on the east face of the base, but the rest of the cross is decorated with interlace and ornamental motifs. The cross is 3.55 m high.

## Killaloe, Co. Clare

See map pages 110–11, square F4

IN THE TOWN CENTRE; O.S. ½" MAP 18.R-703.728

Attached to the inner west wall of the Church of Ireland Cathedral at Killaloe is a twelfth-century limestone cross, 4.20 m high, which Bishop Mant brought from Kilfenora (page 75) in 1821. The head of the cross bears a figure of *the crucified Christ*.

On the floor nearby is a fragment of the upper part of the shaft of a cross (11th/12th century?), with a crude figure (*the crucified Christ?*) on one face. On the other face is a runic inscription, stating that the cross was carved by Thorgrim while, on the side, an Ogham inscription asks for a prayer for Thorgrim. Was Thorgrim a christianised Viking, or a local stonemason with a Viking parent?

## Killamery, Co. Kilkenny

See map pages 110–11, square G5

8.5 KM SOUTH-WEST OF CALLAN; O.S. ½" MAP 18.S-377.360

In the old churchyard close to the Callan-Clonmel road is a sandstone cross, 3.25 m high, which bears animal and marigold decoration on the east face. A panel on the bottom of the west face seems once to have contained an inscription, which Macalister considered to have included the name Maelsechnaill (the high king of Ireland who reigned from 846 to 862?) – though no one else has ever been able to make anything of the inscription.

Above the whorl at the centre of the head of the west face is a panel showing one figure holding a child as another approaches from the right – perhaps *Adam and Eve at Labour*.

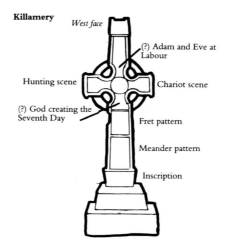

Killamery

West face

(?) Adam and Eve at Labour

Hunting scene

Chariot scene

(?) God creating the Seventh Day

Fret pattern

Meander pattern

Inscription

*Killamery - Head of East face*

Beneath the whorl is a figure flanked by angels, possibly *God creating the Seventh Day,* the day of rest, the two possibly providing an illustration of the old Irish law of Sunday observance. The hunting scenes on the arms of the cross would appear to be unrelated.

Of particular interest on this cross are the scenes on the ends of the arms. On the south arm is *Noah in his Ark,* often taken to be a symbol of baptism. It is not surprising, therefore, that the end of the other arm has a number of scenes which are best interpreted as illustrating events in the life of St John the Baptist. They form four quadrants of a square, as follows: (top left): two figures embracing, probably *Christ and John the Baptist;* (top right): *Herodias,* in the centre, *carries the head of John the Baptist* on the right, while her daughter *Salome dances on her head* on the left; (bottom left): in the middle is the tablet on which *Zacharias* (left) *writes the name of his son John* with a long stylus-pen, which he holds up in his right hand; (bottom right): two figures, that on the left apparently holding a child, probably representing *Zacharias and Elizabeth bringing the infant John the Baptist to the Temple* for his circumcision. This cross may thus have two totally different themes, the seventh day of rest after six days of labour, and the importance of the sacrament of baptism.

## Killary, Co. Meath

See map pages 110–11, square D6

15.5 KM NORTH OF NAVAN; O.S. ½" MAP 13.N-879.830

In the isolated churchyard overlooking the valley of Killary Water there is the shaft of a sandstone cross decorated with a number of biblical scenes, as follows:

**East face** (with the carvings unframed)
1. *Adam and Eve knowing their nakedness.*
2. *Noah's Ark,* which formed the basis for the current logo of the Allied Irish Bank.

*Noah's Ark on the east face of Killary Cross*

3. *The Sacrifice of Isaac,* who bends his head over an altar.
4. *Daniel in the Lions' Den,* above which there is the fragment of an unidentifiable scene.

### North side

On the bottom is, perhaps, *David carrying the head of Goliath,* but what the figure near the top is carrying cannot be made out.

**West face** (overlooking the valley)
1. *The angel announces the birth of Christ to a shepherd,* whose three sheep are shown above one another in the middle.
2. *The Baptism of Christ in the Jordan,* which emanates from two sources – the Jor and the Dan – on the bottom left, and flows between the legs of Christ and John the Baptist.
3. *The Adoration of the Magi,* who are shown above and

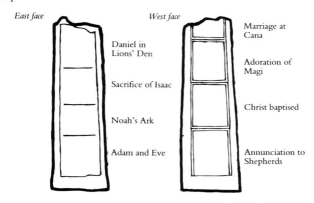

East face — West face

Daniel in Lions' Den

Sacrifice of Isaac

Noah's Ark

Adam and Eve

Marriage at Cana

Adoration of Magi

Christ baptised

Annunciation to Shepherds

beside the Virgin with the Christ child on her lap. The star is shown as a boss between the heads of the two Magi above the Virgin.

4. A fragment of *The Marriage Feast of Cana,* recognisable through the water jars at the bottom of the panel.

★ ★ ★

The selection of biblical scenes on this cross helps to link it with the crosses in the north of Ireland. The New Testament panels show some of the 'firsts' in Christ's life − the first public announcement of his birth, his first presentation to the Gentiles and his first miracle, together with his baptism, which is emphasised by being placed out of its proper chronological order, so that it could be better seen by those kneeling in front of the cross.

There is also another cross-head and base in the church-yard, and a further fragment with damaged and unidenti-fiable figured scenes was discovered in 1986 and brought to the National Museum in Dublin.

## Killeany, Inishmore, Aran Islands, Co. Galway

See map pages 110-11, square F2

2 KM SOUTH-EAST OF KILRONAN; O.S. ½" MAP 14.L-887.072

Placed up against the interior west wall of St Enda's church at Killeany are three fragments of one or two limestone crosses, to which another fragment in a field below the Round Tower also belongs. The lowest of the three fragments in the church has been built in upside down. The only figure sculpture consists of a horseman and parts of a robed figure of *Christ*.

From the same site, but now preserved at Kilronan, is a fragment which was found by Conleth Manning in his excavations in 1984. On one face is a *Crucifixion*.

## (Killesher), Enniskillen, Co. Fermanagh

See map pages 110-11, square C4

IN THE TOWN OF ENNISKILLEN; O.S. ½" MAP 8.H-231.442

In the County Museum in Enniskillen is the head of a sandstone cross from Killesher, which has a *Christ* figure with outstretched arms on one face.

## (Killinaboy), Corofin, Co. Clare

See map pages 110-11, square F3

IN THE CLARE HERITAGE CENTRE IN COROFIN; O.S. ½" MAP 14.R-285.887

Formerly at Killinaboy, but now in the Clare Heritage Centre in Corofin, is a tau- or T-shaped twelfth-century limestone cross with a head on the upper side of each arm. The identification of these heads is problematical, but they could perhaps represent Saints Paul and Anthony, as the latter's attribute is a T-shaped staff.

## Kilnaruane, Co. Cork

See map pages 110-11, square J2

1.5 KM SOUTH-WEST OF BANTRY; O.S. ½" MAP 24.V-985.475

In a field not far from the back of Bantry House is the shaft of a cross, 2.15 m high. The central feature on the east face is an equal-armed cross. Beneath it is a scene of *the raven bringing bread to the desert hermits Paul and Anthony* with, between them, a T-shape which could represent a table or the staff in the form of a T, which is an attribute of St Anthony. Above the cross is an unidentified figure raising its hand in supplication or prayer.

Placed vertically on the west face is a boat with crosses, which was one of the models used by Tim Severin when designing his St Brendan boat with which he crossed the Atlantic in 1976-77. The boat has four oarsmen, another man steering at the stern, while another seated in the prow could represent *Christ stilling the tempest,* a subject surely suitable for a cross exposed to the harsh south-west winds coming from the Atlantic. Above the boat panel are four animals, also vertical, but facing the opposite direction.

## Kilree, Co. Kilkenny

See map pages 110-11, square G5

15 KM SOUTH OF KILKENNY; O.S. ½" MAP 19.S-497.409

The sandstone cross stands to a height of 2.65 m in a field to the west of the church and Round Tower at Kilree. Other than a hunting scene on the arms of the east face and a probable *Adoration of the Magi* on the west face of the head, its only figure sculpture is on the end of the north arm which, as at Killamery (page 79), is divided into four quadrants. A lion can be seen in the top right quadrant, but the identity of the figures in the other three quadrants can not be ascertained satisfactorily.

## Kilronan, Inishmore, Aran Islands –

See map pages 110-11, square F2

SEE UNDER KILLEANY (PAGE 81)

## Kinnitty, Co. Offaly

See map pages 110-11, square F4

14 KM EAST OF BIRR; O.S. ½" MAP 15.N-202.057

Standing in the grounds of the former Forestry School at Castlebernard is a High Cross of sandstone, considered to have been erected originally on the site of a monastery at Kinnitty or Drumcullin (page 52), nearby. The cross, 3.15 m high, has attained new prominence through Dómhnall Ó Murchadha's recent decipherment of the inscriptions on the bottom of both faces of the shaft, indicating that the cross was erected by the high king Maelsechnaill (otherwise Maelsechlainn or Malachy), who reigned from 846 to 862. The incriptions, as read by Ó Murchadha, are as follows:

*Kinnitty - South face*

83

**South face**

OR DO RIG MAELSECHNAILL M MAELRUANAID
OROIT AR RIG HERENN

(A prayer for king Maelsechnaill, son of Maelruanaid
A prayer for the king of Ireland).

**North face**

OR DO COLMAN DORRO . . . IN CROSSA AR RIG
HERENN OR DO RIG HERENN

(A prayer for Colman who made the cross for the king of
Ireland. A prayer for the king of Ireland).

On the north face of the cross, the only figured scene
shows *Eve handing the apple to Adam*. The south face has a
*Crucifixion* at the centre of the head. On the shaft is a scene
which may represent *David playing his lyre* as he is summoned
by a staff-bearing shepherd.

## Lisnaskea, Co. Fermanagh   See map pages 110-11, square C5

IN THE TOWN CENTRE; O.S. ½" MAP 8.H-364.340

The sandstone cross-shaft removed from an unknown site to
its present location in the old potato market in the centre of
Lisnaskea bears *Adam and Eve* on one face, and a series of
bosses on the other.

## Lorrha, Co. Tipperary   See map pages 110-11, square F4

7 KM EAST OF PORTUMNA; O.S. ½" MAP 15.M-920.046

In the grounds of the Church of Ireland church in Lorrha
there are the bases and fragmentary shafts of two sandstone
crosses which have links with Ahenny (page 15) and the
South Cross at Clonmacnois (page 42).

### NORTH-WEST CROSS

The figure sculpture on the fragmentary shaft and on two
faces of the base of this cross is, sadly, so worn that its
subject-matter can no longer be identified. In a long panel at
the bottom of the east face of the base (looking towards the
church) there appear to be a man and a lion facing one
another on the right, and two lions fighting further to the
left. The significance of the panel eludes us, but it is similar
to a panel on the east face of the base of Muiredach's Cross at
Monasterboice (page 86). An animal procession winds its
way around all four sides of the second step of the base.

### SOUTH-EAST CROSS

The mutilated base of this cross bore figure sculpture, none
of it now identifiable save for a possible *Daniel in the Lions
Den* on the north side. There would appear to be a horseman
in a panel on the east face of the cross.

## Monaincha, Co. Tipperary See map pages 110-11, square F5

3 KM EAST-SOUTH-EAST OF ROSCREA;
O.S. ½" MAP 15.S-169.883

On the fragmentary twelfth-century cross re-erected outside
the west end of the Romanesque church at Monaincha,
there is a figure of *the crucified Christ* on the west face of the
head, and the heads of two figures at the bottom of the
north-side of the head-fragment. There are also horsemen on
one side of the base.

## Monasterboice, Co. Louth See map pages 110-11, square D6

8 KM NORTH-WEST OF DROGHEDA;
O.S. ½" MAP 13.O-043.820

Together with Kells in Co. Meath (page 65), Monasterboice represents one of the most important centres in
Ireland for High Crosses, as it has two of the most
significant and best preserved sandstone examples in the
country, both with a rich iconographical programme. In
addition, there are fragments of other crosses on the site,
and further fragments are preserved (but not displayed) in
the National Museum in Dublin.

The place gets its name from the monastery of Buite, a
saint reputed to have prophesied the greatness of St Columba
who, according to an old tradition, was born on the same
day that St Buite died in the year 521. This connection with
St Columba might help to explain a certain similarity in the
sculptural style of the Monasterboice crosses with those
standing in the grounds of the Columban foundation at Kells
in the neighbouring county of Meath. Monasterboice was
occupied for a time by the Vikings until they were attacked
by Domhnall, king of Tara, in 968, and the monastery
remained in existence until at least 1122. Its most visible
monument is the Round Tower, which stands to a height of
28.50 m or just over ninety feet. The loss of its cap may have
been the result of a disastrous fire in 1097, in which some of
the monastery's books and treasures perished. The site also
preserves two late medieval churches which may have served
the pilgrims who came to venerate the relics of St Buite,
which survived down to the Reformation.

### MUIREDACH'S CROSS

The first cross which the visitor meets on entering the old
monastic site from the road is Muiredach's Cross, standing to
a height of about 5.20 m. It gets its modern name from an
inscription on the bottom of the west face of the shaft which
tells us simply that Muireadach had the cross erected. More

85

than one abbot named Muiredach is associated with Monasterboice, but it has not yet proved possible to link the cross to either of them, as there is always the possibility (if not, indeed, the probability) that the cross might have been erected by someone other than an abbot. The two main faces of the cross bear most of the figured panels, though biblical scenes do 'spill over' on to the sides.

**East face** (looking towards the road)

*Base*

The upper register has two figures which seem to be wrestling on their knees, but the lower register is decorated with a panel of interlace.

**Monasterboice – Muiredach's Cross**

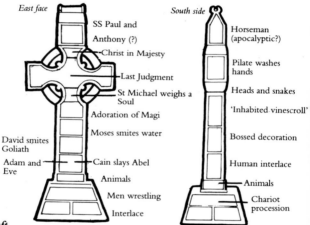

*East face*
- SS Paul and Anthony (?)
- Christ in Majesty
- Last Judgment
- St Michael weighs a Soul
- Adoration of Magi
- Moses smites water
- David smites Goliath
- Adam and Eve
- Cain slays Abel
- Animals
- Men wrestling
- Interlace

*South side*
- Horseman (apocalyptic?)
- Pilate washes hands
- Heads and snakes
- 'Inhabited vinescroll'
- Bossed decoration
- Human interlace
- Animals
- Chariot procession

*Shaft*

Above two animals (lions?) facing one another are:

1. A conflation of *Eve gives the apple to Adam* and *Cain slays Abel.*
2. *David* (second from the left) *departs from an enthroned Saul* on the extreme left, and – armed with his sling, bag of stones and staff – he is seen to have smitten the giant *Goliath* who, even on his knees, is taller than David. The figure on the right is probably one of Goliath's attendants.
3. *Moses* holds up a stick and *smites water from the rock in Horeb,* from which the Israelites drink.
4. *The Adoration of the Magi* with four rather than the usual three Magi.

*Head*

Above *St Michael weighing a soul,* with a devil attempting to upset the balance of the scales in his own favour, is one of the

*Monasterboice, Muiredach's Cross – East face*

most grandiose representations of *The Last Judgment* to survive anywhere in Europe from the first millennium A.D. Christ, with cross-staff and sceptre, and an eagle above his head, is flanked on one side by David with a bird (inspiration in the form of the Holy Spirit) standing on his harp, beside whom an angel records the judgments in a book. Behind David's back are the good souls, facing Christ. On the other side of Christ is David's flute-playing musician, and behind his back a devil with a trident pushes to their eternal damnation those souls who have turned their backs on Christ. Above the Judgment scene is *Christ in Majesty,* flanked by two angels. The top of the cross has the shape of a house or shrine with shingled roof. The figured scene it bears cannot be interpreted satisfactorily, but it may relate to the desert hermits *Paul and Anthony* (who are also present around the corner on the north side).

## South side

### Base
A chariot procession.

### Shaft
Two animals back to back (significance unknown), human interlace, bossed decoration and the 'inhabited vinescroll'.

*Monasterboice, Muiredach's Cross,—Animals under south arm.*

### Head
Under the ring, snakes entwine human heads, and there are two animals beneath the arm. The only panels with human figures are *Pilate washing his hands* on the end of the arm, and a horseman and an angel (apocalyptic?) on the top of the shaft.

## West face

### Base
Fret pattern, interlace and animals.

### Shaft

Between two playful cats bringing in a domestic element – one licking its kitten and the other devouring a bird – is the inscription mentioned above:

OR DO MUIREDACH LASNDERNAD . . . RO

A prayer for Muiredach who had (the cross) erected.

Above the inscription are the following panels:

**Monasterboice – Muiredach's Cross**

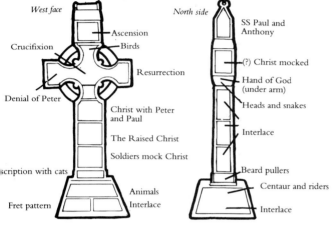

*West face*

- Ascension
- Crucifixion
- Birds
- Resurrection
- Denial of Peter
- Christ with Peter and Paul
- The Raised Christ
- Soldiers mock Christ
- Inscription with cats
- Animals
- Fret pattern
- Interlace

*North side*

- SS Paul and Anthony
- (?) Christ mocked
- Hand of God (under arm)
- Heads and snakes
- Interlace
- Beard pullers
- Centaur and riders
- Interlace

1. *The Second Mocking of Christ/Ecce Rex Iudaeorum.* Christ carries the rod and wears the purple/scarlet cloak (pinned by a penannular brooch, like the Tara brooch) which were given to him by the Roman soldiers as they mock him, calling him King of the Jews (see page 90).
2. *The Raised Christ,* a scene not specifically described in the Bible, showing the Saviour flanked by Saints Peter and Paul, their feet on blocks to suggest that they are above the earth.
3. A scene known as the *Traditio Clavium,* in which Christ is seen to hand a key (*clavium*) to St Peter and the Book of the New Testament to Paul, who has a curious winged creature above his head.

### Head

*The Crucifixion.* Christ is flanked by the figure of *Stephaton* with his sponge, and *Longinus,* whose lance pierces Christ's left side. Between them are small bossed heads, representing the Sun and Moon. Behind Stephaton is a small, outward-facing figure probably representing *Tellus/Ocean* (or, much less likely, *Ecclesia,* the church), who is balanced by a

*Monasterboice, Muiredach's Cross - Inscription and Mocking of Christ*

kneeling figure behind Longinus which must correspondingly represent *Gaia/Earth*, with her small child (or, much less likely, *Synagoga*). The left (north) arm probably illustrates *The Denial of Peter*, while the right (south) arm shows Christ, assisted by angels, rising above two soldiers guarding the tomb at *The Resurrection*. The top of the cross bears *The Ascension of Christ*.

## North side

### Base
Hunting scene with horsemen and centaurs.

### Shaft
Above two men pulling each other's beards (possibly signifying discord) are three beautifully-executed panels of interlace of differing designs.

### Head
The lower side of the ring has heads enmeshed by snakes, as on the south side. Under the arm is *The Hand of God*, emanating from a circle of clouds. The end of the arm bears a scene more likely to be *The First Mocking of Christ* than *The Flagellation*. The top of the shaft shows the raven bringing the loaf to the desert hermits *Paul and Anthony* (with a chalice, of

eucharistic significance, between their feet), placed within the gable of the house-shaped shrine-like structure.

★ ★ ★

One of the major themes on this cross is *Christ the King,* as illustrated on the west face. The bottom panel shows Christ as King of the earth, mocked by the soldiers as the earthly king of the Jews, while the *Crucifixion* represents him as king of the Cosmos, symbolised by the ring, and supported by the presence of earth, ocean, sun and moon. This is further emphasised by *The Raised Christ* showing him as Lord of the skies, while the unusual presence of four rather than the usual three Magi on the east face indicates the four corners of the earth, to whom the infant Christ is presented for the first time. Both earth and heaven are symbolised in the *Traditio Clavium,* with Paul receiving the Gospels and Peter the keys of the kingdom of heaven. Another very important theme is the *Passion, Death and Resurrection of Christ,* illustrated on the head of the west face and spilling over on to the arms on the narrow sides. *The Last Judgment* occupies the centre of the head on the east face, the ultimate climax in a series of events initiated by *Adam and Eve* on the bottom panel of the shaft. They share the panel with their children *Cain and Abel,* the latter the first innocent victim of the Old Testament, pre-figuring Christ as the innocent victim in the New Testament. *David overcoming Goliath* symbolises the victory of good over evil, while *Moses striking water from the rock* is one of those Old Testament events chosen for illustration on the Irish crosses to show how God helps his faithful followers from death (in this instance, from thirst in the desert). Through St Paul's letter to the Corinthians (1, 10.4), the scene is linked with the waters of life flowing from the side of Christ in the *Crucifixion,* providing it with a eucharistic significance indicated also by the chalice at the feet of *Saints Paul and Anthony,* the hermits, at the top of the north side. Thus, the complicated web of themes on this cross can be seen to include not only *Christ as Lord of the Earth and the Cosmos,* but also his *Passion, Death, Resurrection and Ascension,* as well as the *Eucharist.*

## THE TALL, OR WEST CROSS

Standing close to the Round Tower is the tallest High Cross in the country, standing to a height of over 7 m, or twenty-one feet. Its height allows it to have more scenes than any other cross in Ireland, despite the lack of figure sculpture on the base.

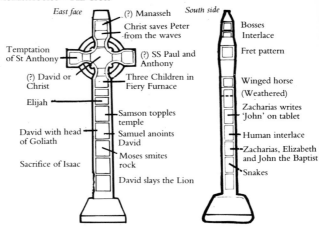

East face — labels: (?) Manasseh; Christ saves Peter from the waves; Temptation of St Anthony; (?) SS Paul and Anthony; (?) David or Christ; Three Children in Fiery Furnace; Elijah; Samson topples temple; David with head of Goliath; Samuel anoints David; Sacrifice of Isaac; Moses smites rock; David slays the Lion.

South side — labels: Bosses; Interlace; Fret pattern; Winged horse (Weathered); Zacharias writes 'John' on tablet; Human interlace; Zacharias, Elizabeth and John the Baptist; Snakes.

## East face

### Shaft

1. *David slays the lion.*
2. *The Sacrifice of Isaac.*
3. *Moses smites water from the rock in Horeb* (as on the east face of Muiredach's Cross).
4. A conflation of *David with the head of Goliath* and *Samuel anointing David*.
5. *Samson toppling the pillar of the house* or temple, in the presence of the Philistines.
6. *Elijah ascends to heaven* in his chariot.

### Head

Above a panel of interlace, we see *The Three Children in the Fiery Furnace*, fuelled by the faggots brought by soldiers. The centre of the head is occupied by *David being acclaimed king of Israel* or *The Second Coming of Christ*. On the south (left) arm is *The Temptation of St Anthony, the hermit* by beasts, while the other arm may show him and his friend St *Paul* dealing with an upside-down devil who has come to tempt them. The uppermost limb of the cross shows the miracle of *Christ saving St Peter from the waves*, above which is probably the Old Testament figure of *Manasseh* offering the sacrifice of a bull as he removes a circular grove which he had earlier set up in honour of a false god.

## South side

### Shaft

The only two figured scenes both probably illustrate St John the Baptist. The lower of the two is likely to show *Zacharias, with Elizabeth carrying the infant John the Baptist*, while the

*Monasterboice, Tall Cross - Head of East face*

upper one represents *Zacharias writing the name John on a tablet.* There is a fabulous beast just beneath the ring on the head of the cross.

## West face

### Shaft

1. A much-abraded scene showing *Christ in the Tomb,* with soldiers asleep on the tomb-slab covering the prostrate body of Christ.

**Monasterboice – Tall Cross**

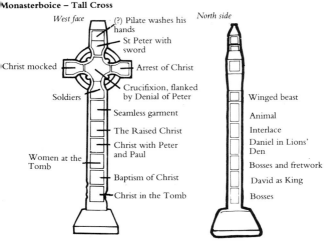

*West face*
- (?) Pilate washes his hands
- St Peter with sword
- Christ mocked
- Arrest of Christ
- Soldiers
- Crucifixion, flanked by Denial of Peter
- Seamless garment
- The Raised Christ
- Christ with Peter and Paul
- Women at the Tomb
- Baptism of Christ
- Christ in the Tomb

*North side*
- Winged beast
- Animal
- Interlace
- Daniel in Lions' Den
- Bosses and fretwork
- David as King
- Bosses

2. *The Baptism of Christ,* with the Saviour half immersed in the Jordan.

The other panels each contain three figures, not all of whom are easy to identify, but the following interpretations may be suggested:

3. *The Three Holy Women coming to the Tomb,* bearing spices.
4. *Traditio Clavium* (as on Muiredach's Cross), with Christ handing the keys to St Peter and the New Testament to St Paul.
5. *The Raised Christ* (also as on Muiredach's Cross).
6. *The soldiers casting lots for Christ's seamless garment.*

### Head

In the centre, two soldiers support *the crucified Christ,* with *Stephaton* and *Longinus* flanked by the heads of the Sun and the Moon. *The Denial of Peter* is split into two sections on either side of The Crucifixion, that beside Christ's left hand showing St Peter warming his hands over a brazier, with a cock above, while beside Christ's right hand is another cock, and the maidservant raising her hand questioning Peter as to whether he knew Christ. Behind her is probably a *Flagellation* or, more likely, *The First Mocking of Christ,* balanced on the end of the other arm by *The Kiss of Judas,* with a soldier approaching from the left to arrest Christ as he is embraced by Judas. Above the head of the crucified Christ, *Peter draws his sword,* prior to cutting off the ear of Malchus (who is not shown). On top is a much-worn scene possibly representing *Pilate washing his hands,* though it could conceivably be *Christ before the Sanhedrin.*

### North side

The figured panels on this side represent *David as King* and *Daniel in the Lions' Den,* again with a fabulous beast beneath the ring – a griffin which, being half lion (the king of earthly animals) and half eagle (lord of the skies), usually symbolises *Christ as the Lord of the earth and the skies.*

\* \* \*

One of the many surprises on this cross is that the two main faces do not show the Bible scenes in their correct scriptural order. This is particularly noticeable in the case of each of the bottom panels and, in the case of the west face, it is perhaps explained by the desire to show Christ's greatest victory at the moment of *Resurrection* from the tomb to those who would have been kneeling in prayer in front of the cross. The placing of David slaying the lion on the bottom of the east face may have been intended to draw attention to the *glorification of David* as one of the main themes on the shaft and (?) head above it. Other themes demonstrated are how God helped the faithful in times of danger – the innocent *Isaac,* the *thirsting Israelites* and the *Three Children in the Fiery Furnace* – and those who called upon the Lord for help in their hour of need, as instanced by the long-haired *Samson* and the rather more unexpected Old Testament figure of *Manassēh.* Some of the themes on this cross – and even a few of the actual scenes chosen to illustrate them – are similar to those on Muiredach's Cross – the desert hermits *Paul and Anthony,* and the *Passion, Death and Resurrection of Christ.* One unusual scene, shown here beneath the Crucifixion, is *The soldiers with Christ's seamless garment,* which symbolises the indivisibility of the church. Indirectly related to it is the predilection of subjects concerning the Prince of the Apostles – *St Peter drawing his sword, the Denial, Christ saving Peter from the waters* and the *Traditio Clavium* – suggesting a considerable influence from Rome in the source of the iconography on this cross. A baptismal emphasis may also be presumed through the location low down on the shaft of the west face of *The Baptism* and the presence on the south side of two scenes from the childhood cycle of *St John the Baptist,* instead of the Adoration of the Magi from the childhood of Christ cycle on Muiredach's Cross.

### NORTH CROSS

In an enclosure near the north-eastern corner of the churchyard is the head of a third cross which bears a *Crucifixion* on its west face. Close to it is the shaft of a further cross bearing at least one scene so worn as to be unrecognisable.

## Moone, Co. Kildare   See map pages 110-11, square F6

7.5 KM NORTH OF CASTLEDERMOT; O.S. ½" MAP 16.S-789.927

In an old graveyard, which is on the site of a probable Columban monastery, there are two crosses – one tall, the other incomplete – and the base of a third cross.

### TALL CROSS

This cross is unique in Ireland not only for its tall, thin shape, but also for the graphic, naive charm of the carved panels on the base, where almost all of the figure sculpture is concentrated. The cross consists of three parts which were re-erected together in 1893, totalling a height of 7.04 m, thus making it the second tallest High cross in the country after the West Cross at Monasterboice.

**East face** (not visible from the entrance to the graveyard).

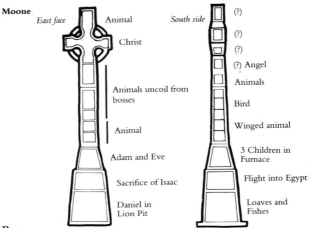

**Moone**

East face — Animal — Christ — Animals uncoil from bosses — Animal — Adam and Eve — Sacrifice of Isaac — Daniel in Lion Pit

South side — (?) — (?) — (?) — (?) Angel — Animals — Bird — Winged animal — 3 Children in Furnace — Flight into Egypt — Loaves and Fishes

*Base*

1. *Daniel in the Lion Pit.* The fact that there are seven lions rather than the usual two or four shows that this is not the more common *Daniel in the Lions' Den,* when Daniel was thrown into the den during the reign of the Persian king Darius, but rather the scene when he was thrown into the pit with seven lions during the reign of the preceding monarch, Cyrus, as related in the apocryphal part of the Book of Daniel known as 'Bel and the Dragon'.
2. *The Sacrifice of Isaac.*
3. *Adam and Eve.*

*Cross*

On the shaft there are contorting animals, as well as bosses. On the head is a figure which must be *Christ,* but (presuming that the cross was correctly re-assembled in 1893) not the crucified Christ, as there is a Crucifixion on the west face of the base.

### South side

On the base are:

1. *The Miracle of the Loaves and Fishes,* without the figure of Christ.
2. *The Flight into Egypt,* with Joseph pulling the reluctant, yet happy-looking, pony bearing the Virgin and Child. The presence of the head of Christ at a diagonal to the Virgin strongly suggests that Christ's body must originally have been painted over the Virgin's body.
3. *The Three Children in the Fiery Furnace.*

*Moone - South side of base*

The single figures on the head-fragment of the cross cannot be identified.

**West face** (opposite the entrance to the graveyard)
*The Twelve Apostles* stand beneath *The Crucifixion* on the base. There are animals on the shaft of the cross, but the figures on the ends of the arms cannot be identified.

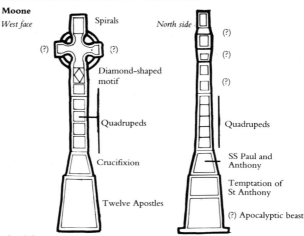

**Moone**
*West face* — Spirals
(?)       (?)
Diamond-shaped motif
Quadrupeds
Crucifixion
Twelve Apostles

*North side*
(?)
(?)
(?)
Quadrupeds
SS Paul and Anthony
Temptation of St Anthony
(?) Apocalyptic beast

## North side
The three panels on the base represent:
1. Seven-headed monster (presumably of the Apocalypse).
2. *The Temptation of St Anthony the hermit.*
3. A ponderous raven flies above the heads of *the desert hermits Paul and Anthony,* but there is no sign of the bread which he brought them.

The single figures on the head fragment remain unidentified.

★ ★ ★

One theme on this beautiful cross is the Help of God – how God assisted those who were faithful to him in their hour of need. This is illustrated from the Old Testament in the case of *Isaac, Daniel* and the *Three Children,* but also from the New Testament through *the Christ child* who would otherwise have been slaughtered by Herod, and *the multitude* who would have hungered had not Christ performed the *Miracle of the Loaves and Fishes.* It will be noticed that, on the sides of the base containing these scenes, the chronological order goes from top to bottom. This was doubtless so that the figures of *Adam and Eve* should be placed back-to-back with *The Crucifixion,* to show that the latter was a consequence of the former, Adam and Eve being differentiated from the other scenes by being carved in a more rounded relief. It will be noted, too, that there is a neat relationship between the middle panels on the east and south faces of the base, in that it is a child in each instance which has been saved by the appearance of the Lord's angel.

**FRAGMENTARY CROSS**
The path leading from the road to the Tall Cross passes through a ruined medieval church in which fragments of a further cross have been mounted in cement. Its decoration consists not only of bosses and spiral ornament, but also animals, one with long, floppy ears of basset-hound proportions so similar to an animal on the Tall Cross that the same master-mason is likely to have been responsible for the carving of both crosses. A recently-discovered shaft-fragment, now in the keeping of Kildare County Council, bears a mutilated horseman.

## Newtown, Co. Carlow     See map pages 110-11, square G6
11 KM SOUTH-SOUTH-EAST OF CARLOW;
O.S. ½" MAP 19.S-751.633

Built into a road fence in the townland of Kildreenagh are the head and probable base of a granite cross. On one face of the head there is apparently a *Crucifixion,* and a probable *David playing the harp.*

## Oldcourt, Co. Wicklow     See map pages 110-11, square F7
1 KM SOUTH OF BRAY; O.S. ½" MAP 16.O-262.176

In a private demesne at Oldcourt there is a granite base, comparable to that at Moone (page 95), and which is said to have been found nearby in the early nineteenth century. Elucidation of the carvings has been made more difficult by weathering, though *Adam and Eve* are discernible on the west face, and *St Michael weighing souls* as well as *Daniel in the Lions' Den* on the east face.

## Old Kilcullen, Co. Kildare     See map pages 110-11, square F6
2.5 KM SOUTH-WEST OF KILCULLEN;
O.S. ½" MAP 16.N-829.070

On the prominent monastic site at Old Kilcullen, with its Round Tower on a hill-top, there are the shafts of two granite crosses, and an undecorated base. The taller (eastern) of the two shafts appears to have borne sculpture, but this is now so worn as to be no longer recognisable.

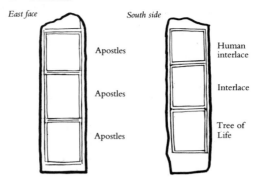

*East face* — Apostles / Apostles / Apostles

*South side* — Human interlace / Interlace / Tree of Life

## WEST SHAFT

The sculpture on the smaller shaft is better preserved and may be tentatively interpreted as follows:

### East face

Three panels, each with four figures, presumably representing *The Apostles*. Some bear books.

### South side

The south side bears a tree of life guarded by two winged quadrupeds on the bottom, and a human interlace in the top panel.

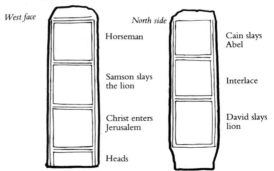

*West face* — Horseman / Samson slays the lion / Christ enters Jerusalem / Heads

*North side* — Cain slays Abel / Interlace / David slays lion

## West face

1. Five heads.
2. Probably *Christ's entry into Jerusalem*.
3. Perhaps *Samson slays the lion*.
4. Horseman.
5. Feet, probably those of *Christ* carved on the missing head.

*Old Kilcullen - North side*

**North side**

1. *David slaying the lion.*
2. A panel of interlace.
3. Probably *Cain slaying his prostrate brother Abel with an axe*. Beside Cain's head is the altar of their sacrifice.

## Roscrea, Co. Tipperary

See map pages 110-11, square F4

IN THE TOWN CENTRE; O.S. ½" MAP 15.S-137.893

Close to the well-known west gable of St Cronan's church in the centre of the town of Roscrea are two fragments of a cross, mounted together to a height of over 3 m. Weathering has been unkind to the surface of this cross, which must have been one of the finest twelfth-century examples in Ireland.

The figures on the east face of the lower fragment are *Adam and Eve,* but the figures in high relief on the other faces cannot be satisfactorily identified.

The west face of the head (looking out onto the street) is largely occupied by the high relief figure of *the crucified Christ,* while, in the same position on the east face, is a bishop or abbot, probably representing *St Cronan,* the founder of the monastery in Roscrea.

Beside a wall opposite the west doorway of the Catholic church in the town there is a pillar which is decorated on three sides, but – other than animals – the sculptural details are difficult to make out clearly.

## St Mullins, Co. Carlow

See map pages 110-11, square G6

6 KM SOUTH-SOUTH-EAST OF GRAIGUENAMANAGH; O.S. ½" MAP 19.S-729.380

Close to the edge of where the old monastic site of St Mullins drops steeply to the river Barrow below, there are the cylindrical base, the partial shaft and the head of a granite cross. The figure sculpture is confined to the east face of the cross, where there is a *Crucifixion* at the centre of the head. The two figures beneath may well have been *Apostles* (with the other ten having presumably been carved on the lost fragment of the shaft), but the identity of the three figures above, and the surviving figures on the arm and head, cannot be satisfactorily identified.

## Seir Kieran, Co. Offaly

See map pages 110-11, square F4

8.5 KM EAST-SOUTH-EAST OF BIRR; O.S. ½" MAP 15.N-139.022

In the graveyard of Seir Kieran, the site of a fifth-century monastery, there is a decorated base, 75 cm high, which was dug out of the ground in 1937. The only identifiable scenes are on the east face, where they are superimposed in two rows without there being any formal division between the individual subjects. Reading from left to right, the bottom row shows *Nebuchadnezzar* and his soldiers approaching the *Three Children in the Fiery Furnace,* who can be seen being protected by the angel's wing at the bottom of the centre of the panel, and *Adam and Eve* further to the right. The upper row, correspondingly, has (?) *David brings the head of Goliath to Jerusalem, The Sacrifice of Isaac* and, on the top right, two horses. The north face has what seems like a battle scene, with figures bearing staffs facing oncoming horsemen.

## Slane Co. Meath – See map pages 110-11, square E6

SEE UNDER FENNOR (PAGE 61)

## Temple Brecan, Inishmore, Aran Islands, Co. Galway

See map pages 110-11, square F2

8 KM WEST-NORTH-WEST OF KILRONAN;
O.S. ½" MAP 14.L-810.120

In the vicinity of Temple Brecan, near the western end of the Aran island of Inishmore, there are numerous cross-fragments, belonging probably to a total of three crosses. They stand in the churchyard and in an enclosure to the north-east of the church, and two of them bear a *Crucifixion* scene. Like the cross-head from Killeany on the same island (page 81), these Aran Crucifixions are accompanied by the figures of *Stephaton* and *Longinus,* who are otherwise not normally present on the stone High Crosses of the twelfth century, though they do feature on other Irish Crucifixion representations of the period.

## Termonfeckin, Co. Louth See map pages 110-11, square D6

7 KM NORTH-EAST OF DROGHEDA; O.S. ½" MAP 13.O-141.805

The main monument to survive from the monastery founded here by St Feichín in the seventh century is the High Cross standing 2.20 m above a rounded base close to the west door of the Church of Ireland church. In addition to many panels of attractive geometrical decoration, the cross bears a *Crucifixion* on the east face (looking towards the church) and an abbreviated representation of *The Last Judgment* on the west face. The cross is likely to have been re-erected the wrong way round at some stage, as *The Crucifixion* normally faces west (see illustration page 104).

*Termonfeckin - East face*

## Tihilly, Co. Offaly See map pages 110-11, square E5

7 KM NORTH-WEST OF TULLAMORE;
O.S. ½" MAP 15.N-302.290

On the old monastic site at Tihilly, a few hundred metres from the road between Tullamore and Clara, a fragmentary High Cross was reconstructed by Liam de Paor in the 1950s. The cap of the cross is currently housed in the Department of Archaeology in University College, Dublin. Without it, the cross stands to a height of 2.35 m. The figure sculpture is confined to the west face where, above a winged griffin at the bottom of the shaft, *Adam and Eve* stand beneath the branches of the apple tree, and there is a *Crucifixion* at the centre of the head. The selection of these two panels was presumably to stress that it was the Original Sin of our first parents which led Christ to give his life for mankind upon the cross.

## Tory Island, Co. Donegal See map pages 110-11, square A4

11 KM WEST-NORTH-WEST OF HORN HEAD;
O.S. ½" MAP 1.B-857.466

On this island off the north-west coast of County Donegal, there are two fragments of a twelfth-century cross close to the Round Tower at West Town. One face bore the figure of *the crucified Christ* in high relief. The upper fragment now lies loose, while the lower fragment has been inserted upside down in a base. Nearby is the probable fragment of another cross, and near the boat-slip is a tall T-shaped cross.

## Tuam, Co. Galway See map pages 110-11, square E3

IN THE TOWN CENTRE; O.S. ½" MAP 11.M-436.520

Formerly the seat of the O Conors, kings of Connacht, Tuam preserves the remnants of at least four separate sandstone crosses. With the exception of one which is currently in storage in the town, they are all displayed in the Church of Ireland Cathedral.

The so-called Market cross, which stood in the centre of the town until moved to its present location in the south transept in 1992, is made up of the shaft and head of two separate crosses, which did not originally belong together and which, together, now total almost 4 m in height. One face of the head bears a *crucified Christ* wearing a loincloth, while the other shows figures flanking a bishop or abbot, who may represent *St Jarlath*, the founder of the monastery at Tuam. The shaft, which clearly does not fit the head, is decorated with animal interlacing, and its base bears two sets of ecclesiastical figures. On one side of the bottom of the base is

*Tuam Cathedral, Market Cross-South face of head*

an inscription asking for a prayer for Turlough O Conor, and on another side a second inscription requesting a prayer for abbot O hOissin – the high king of Ireland and the abbot of Tuam respectively – which help us to date this cross between the years 1126 and 1152.

Near the western end of the Cathedral is the shaft of another cross which bears no figure sculpture, but has two inscriptions. One, placed horizontally, reads:

OR DON RIG THORDELBUCH U CHONCHOBAR
OR DON THAER GILLU CR U THUATHAIL

A prayer for the king, for Turdelbuch O Conor
A prayer for the wright, Gillu Christ O'Toole

and the other, placed vertically, is as follows:

OR DO CHOMHARBA IARLAITHE DO AED U OSSIN . . .
NDERNAD IN CHROSSA

A prayer for the successor of Jarlath, for Aed O hOssin who had the cross made.

The high king and the abbot are the same personages named in the inscription on the Market Cross mentioned above, but, sadly, we know nothing more of Gillu Christ O'Toole, who must have been the master mason who carved the cross at the behest of abbot O hOssin.

## Tybroughney, Co. Kilkenny
See map pages 110-11, square G5

4 KM EAST OF CARRICK-ON-SUIR; O.S. ½" MAP 22.S-441.216

In an old graveyard close to the railway-line at Tybroughney, otherwise known as Tibberaghney, there is a sandstone shaft which probably formed part of a cross originally. The east face bears spirals, and the others bear fabulous animals, including a centaur, though there are no actual biblical scenes on the fragment.

## Tynan, Co. Armagh
See map pages 110-11, square C6

11 KM WEST-SOUTH-WEST OF ARMAGH;
O.S. ½" MAP 8.H-765.430

In the centre of Tynan village, fragments of two sandstone crosses have been mounted together one on top of the other. The east face of the shaft bears a panel with *Adam and Eve,* while back-to-back with it is a panel which Dr. Ann Hamlin suggests may perhaps represent *Christ's Second Coming.*

There are three further sandstone crosses in a fragmentary state in the grounds of Tynan Abbey estate. One, called the Well Cross, bears a much-worn *Crucifixion* at the centre of the west face, and a probable representation of *the raven bringing bread to Saints Paul and Anthony* beneath it.

## Ullard, Co. Kilkenny
See map pages 110-11, square G5/6

5 KM NORTH-NORTH-EAST OF GRAIGUENAMANAGH;
O.S. ½" MAP 19.S-724.482

Three fragments of a granite cross, linked by a modern cement shaft, stand close to the incongruous ball-alley built on to the eastern end of the Romanesque church at Ullard.

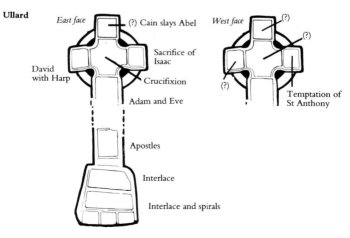

**Ullard**

*East face* — (?) Cain slays Abel

Sacrifice of Isaac

David with Harp — Crucifixion

Adam and Eve

Apostles

Interlace

Interlace and spirals

*West face* — (?)

(?)

(?)

Temptation of St Anthony

**East face**

The base has panels bearing geometrical motifs, while the shaft standing in it has carvings of six figures, presumably *Apostles,* the other six of whom would have been present on the lost fragment originally above it. At the top of the shaft are *Adam and Eve,* above which is *The Crucifixion* at the centre of the head. *David plays his lyre* on the left arm, while *The Sacrifice of Isaac* is shown on the right arm, but the scene on the top is uncertain (*Cain slaying Abel?*).

**West face**

The west face (overlooking the handball alley) is much more heavily worn, and the carvings accordingly difficult to decipher, but they may represent scenes from the lives of the desert hermits *Paul and Anthony.*

*Ullard - Head of east face*

For further reading, consult Peter Harbison,
*The High Crosses of Ireland,* 3 vols., Bonn, 1992.

108

# APPENDIX: CROSSES WITH NO FIGURE SCULPTURE

The following is a list of selected crosses (with map co-ordinates) likely to be earlier than 1200 A.D., but which bear no figure sculpture and were originally more than 1.50 m in height, together with a list of smaller examples with some form of decoration. (★ = with geometrical ornament, or inscribed cross, or inscription, or with cup-and-circle ornament. Those without asterisk are plain.)

★Abbeyshrule, Co. Longford
(12.N-225.593).

Adamstown, Co. Wexford
(19.S-871.277).

Aghanaglack, Co. Fermanagh
(7.H-111.434).

Aghowle, Co. Wicklow
(19.S-931.694).

★Ballinatray Lower, Co. Wexford
(19.T-193.568).

★Ballymore Eustace, Co. Kildare
(16.N-933.099).

★Ballynaguilkee Lower, Co. Waterford
(22.S-182.050).

★Ballynilard, Co. Tipperary
(18.R-866.348).

★Bangor, Co. Down (private)
(5.J-474.796).

★Blessington, Co. Wicklow
(from Burgage More) (16.N-976.135).

★Broghanlea, Co. Antrim (2.D-133.408).

★Caledon, Co. Tyrone (private)
(8.H-753.437).

Carrownaff, Co. Donegal
(2.C-598.383).

★Castlekeeran, Co. Meath
(13.N-690.774).

★Castlewellan Forest Park, Co. Down
(from Drumadonnell) (9.J-336.364).

★Clogher, Co. Tyrone (8.H-537.516).

★Clonfad, Co. Westmeath
(13.N-544.453).

★Clonmore, Co. Carlow (19.S-965.761).

Clontallagh, Co. Donegal (1.C-122.404)

★Delgany, Co. Wicklow
(16.O-276.108).

★Dromore, Co. Down (9.J-200.533).

Drumcolumb, Co. Sligo
(7.G-773.200).

★Eglish, Co. Armagh (8.H-806.502).

★Emlagh, Co. Roscommon
(11.M-699.775).

Emly, Co. Tipperary (18.R-762.346)

★Errigal Keerogue, Co. Tyrone
(8.H-585.570).

★Ferns, Co. Wexford (19.T-021.498).

★Finglas, Co. Dublin (16.O-132.389).

Fore, Co. Westmeath
(13.N-509.703).

★Garryhundon, Co. Carlow
(19.S-723.692).

★Inishkeel, Co. Donegal (3.B-710.001)

Inishmacsaint, Co. Fermanagh
(7.H-165.541).

★Kilbroney, Co. Down (9.J-187.195).

★Kilcashel, Co. Donegal (3.G-693.929).

Killiney, Co. Kerry (20.Q-607.127).

★Killoan, Co. Tyrone (4.H-297.753).

★Kilmainham, Co. Dublin
(16.O-129.339).

★Kilmalkedar, Co. Kerry
(20.Q-403.062).

★Kilmokea, Co. Wexford
(23.S-686.164).

★Kilquiggin, Co. Wicklow
(19.S-961.716).

★Kilteel, Co. Kildare (16.N-984.213).

★Leggettsrath, Co. Kilkenny
(19.S-535.557).

★Lismore, Co. Waterford
(22.X-048.986).

Magharees, Co. Kerry (20.Q-622.212).

★Monaghan County Museum,
Co. Monaghan (from Selloo)
(8.H-672.329).

Mullaboy, Co. Derry (2.C-512.131).

★Noughaval, Co. Clare (14.R-206.967).

★Nurney, Co. Carlow (19.S-734.674).

Old Leighlin, Co. Carlow
(19.S-658.654).

★Orchard, Co. Carlow (19.S-702.672).

★Ray, Co. Donegal (1.B-955.337).

★Reenconnell, Co. Kerry
(20.Q-424.063).

★Sleaty, Co. Laois (19.S-714.791).

★Taghmon, Co. Wexford
(23.S-918.197).

★Tonaknock, Co. Kerry
(17.Q-844.269).

★Toureen Peakaun, Co. Tipperary
(18.S-004.284).

Tullaghan, Co. Leitrim (3.G-787.577).

★Tullaghore, Co. Antrim
(2.D-096.339).

★Tullow, Co. Carlow (19.S-852.729).

Tully, Co. Dublin (16.O-234.235).

Waterstown, Co. Carlow
(19.S-886.827).

# Irish
# High Crosses

with figure sculptures

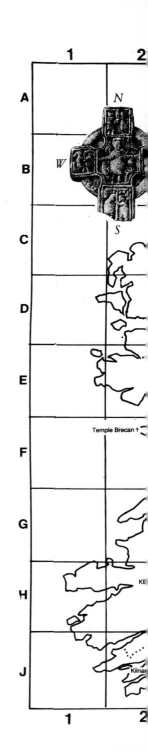

N

W

S

Temple Brecan †

KE

Kilna

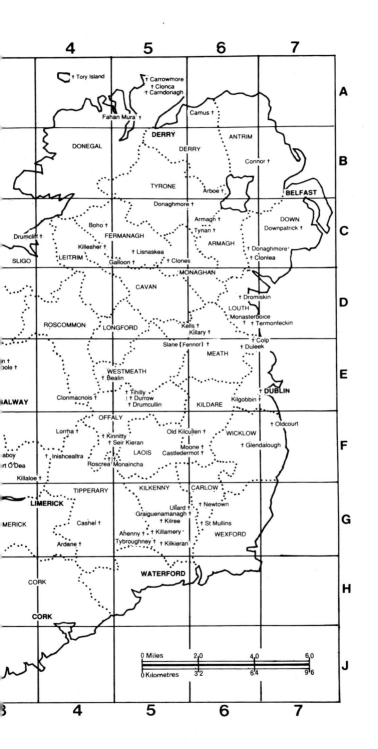